FLOWERS

& No More Medea

by
Deborah Porter

Playwrights Canada Press
Toronto • Canada

Flowers © 1993 *No More Medea* © 1990 Deborah Porter
Playwrights Canada Press is the publishing imprint of
the Playwrights Union of Canada (PUC): 54 Wolseley St., 2nd fl.,
Toronto, Ontario CANADA M5T lA5
Tel: (416) 947-0201 Fax: (416) 947-0159

Playwrights Canada Press acknowledges the financial assistance
of The Canada Council - Writing and Publishing Section, and Theatre
Section, and the Ontario Arts Council.

Canadian Cataloguing in Publication Data
Porter, Deborah, 1959—
        Flowers; &, No more Medea

Two plays ISBN 0-88754-526-2
I. Title. II Title: No more Medea
PS8581.077F56 1994   C812'.54   C94-930888-9
PR9199.3.P67F56 1994

First edition: August 1994.
Printed and bound in Winnipeg, Manitoba, Canada.

Contents

Introduction

Six years ago at the height of winter, some 15 women and Peter Hinton met in the Backspace of Theatre Passe Muraille, where Deborah Porter was clutching a huge stack of monologues, scenes and paraphernalia in random order. The seed of *Flowers* was thus planted but would take some five years and as many drafts to come to full bloom. Please forgive that rather predictable, extended metaphor. It is meant simply to amuse and disgust Deborah whose perverse sense of humour is born out of her impulse to celebrate contradiction in her writing through irony, parody and various lower, if not outright vulgar, comedic conventions, as witnessed in *No More Medea*. Unlike *Flowers,* this vicious, iconoclastic comedy took Deborah almost no time at all. The initial draft spewed forth in some five days as opposed to years and was produced three months later.

At first glance, it is almost impossible to believe these two plays have anything in common: one is a delicate full-length drama, poetically textured and complexly constructed, the other a snappy, vindictive one act that cuts like a knife. Upon closer inspection, it becomes very clear that both pieces present women struggling to discover and accept their unique female identities in the face of almost insurmountable obstacles.

At the risk of sounding sexist, these plays exemplify the virtues of "female" writing. Both plays communicate primarily the way women do — they "share" their stories with the audience rather than just telling them. The narrative structure is not linear, nor is it the machine that drives the action of these pieces. The basic, psychological movement of these plays is necessarily introspective but articulated in brave presentational sweeps. Finally, in these two works, Deborah has created seven wonderfully different female characters who will live on in the theatre to tell the stories of their lives.

Iris Turcott
Toronto

Flowers

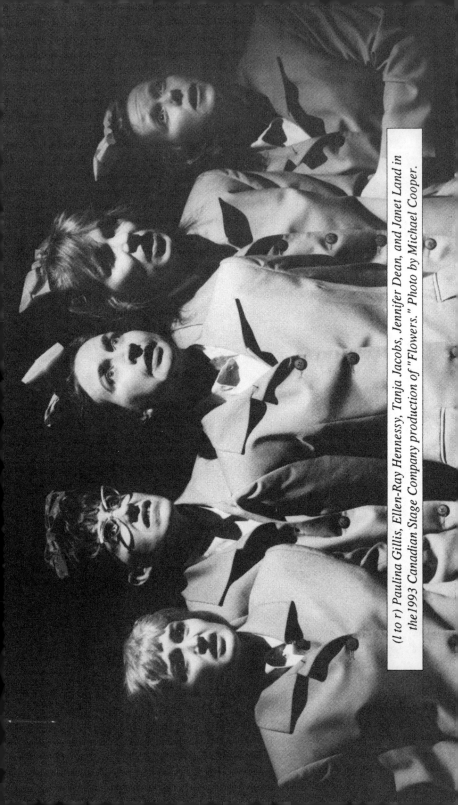

(l to r) Paulina Gillis, Ellen-Ray Hennessy, Tanja Jacobs, Jennifer Dean, and Janet Land in the 1993 Canadian Stage Company production of "Flowers." Photo by Michael Cooper.

For my family

Playwrights Acknowledgements

I would like to thank The Canadian Stage Company, The Grand Theatre, Nightwood Theatre, Theatre Passe Muraille, Necessary Angel Theatre, D.D. Kugler, Lynda Hill, National Archives of Canada - Kathleen Owens, Archives of Ontario, Ontario Arts Council, and all the men and women involved in the development of the play, especially two individuals, Peter Hinton and Iris Turcott, whose ongoing encouragement, expertise and commitment kept me going. Iris Turcott and Charlie Tomlinson were the dramaturgs for the final text.

Special thanks to Jerry Doiron for being there — semper fidelis.

Production history

Flowers premiered at The Canadian Stage Company's Berkeley Street
Theatre, Toronto, January, 1993, with the following cast:

SYLVIE	*Tanja Jacobs*
MARIETTE	*Jennifer Dean*
JOSEE	*Janet Land*
ADELE	*Paulina Gillis*
THERESE	*Ellen-Ray Hennessy*

Directed by Peter Hinton.
Set and costume design by Cecile Belec.
Lighting design by Oliver Merk.
Stage managed by Maria Popoff.
Assistant stage management by Thom Payne.

Flowers was subsequently revised and produced at The Grand Theatre's
McManus Theatre (Undergrand), London, Ontario, January, 1994, with
the following cast:

SYLVIE	*Kim Renders*
MARIETTE	*Pamela Matthews*
JOSEE	*Karen Woolridge*
ADELE	*Catherine Bruhier*
THERESE	*Genevieve Langlois*

Directed by Charlie Tomlinson.
Designed by John Thompson.
Stage managed by Susan McNeil.
Assistant stage management by Anne Marie McConney.
Assistant design by Jennifer Brumer.
Assistant direction by Kristen Van Alphen.

The Characters

The play is performed by five actresses playing the following roles:

SYLVIE PAQUETTE
MARIETTE PAQUETTE
JOSEE PAQUETTE
ADELE PAQUETEE
THERESE PAQUETTE

Doubling of roles:

ETIENNE PAQUETTE, their father, played by Therese.
MANON PAQUETTE, their mother, played by Adele.
GASTON PAQUETTE, their brother, played by Josee.

JOHN DRAPER, their doctor, played by Mariette.
WILLIAM BARKER, another doctor, played by Therese.
RACHEL WINTER, a nurse, played by Josee.
VARIOUS NURSES, played by Josee, Adele, Therese.

MLLE. LALONGE, an art teacher, played by Josee.
A TEACHER, played by Sylvie.

GLORIA SHERIDAN, a reporter, played by Josee.
A REPORTER, played by Adele.
A RADIO HOST, played by Therese.

Playwright's note on doubling of characters

Since the action of the play is conjured by Sylvie, all parts are doubled because she is making transferences. The parents, who are dead, are played by the sisters who are also deceased. Qualities of personality are also transferred, for example, Draper's authoritarian manner is transferred to Mariette who is rebellious. Josee plays characters who are generally more nurturing. Sylvie doubles when she has something to learn by trying on a certain point of view.

The doubling is something to be accomplished primarily by actors taking on behavioural qualities and quirks rather than by costume trickery; they are cameo portraits, drawn by the main characters, capturing the essence of the double. These changes of character are very important to the play, as they represent strong people and influences connected to through words, images, and memories.

Playwrights note on the Chorus

While the doubling of characters reveals individuality, the Chorus operates as a unifying voice, indicating synchronicity of emotion and remembrance. It is meant to show how the group — in reality, a disparate collection of actresses — functions verbally, and at times, physically, as a perfect whole and a singular personality.

The Setting

The play takes place between 1934 and 1970 approximately. The physical world of the play is a dreamscape; the set should be very minimal and suggestive of different environments. Certain elements, like the dressers, which contain identity markers, and chairs are certainly important. A feeling of outdoors, of the smallness of the individual before the universe, is vital.

The Costumes

The five actresses should wear matching clothes. One basic costume, such as a classic suit, can take them through the play. The action of putting on hair bows establishes the characters are girls, removing them suggests an advancement in age. Different costume pieces might be added to clarify action: Sylvie's paint smock, Josee's pregnancy dress, a black sweater for Mariette. Sylvie should wear a habit for her convent scenes.

(l to r) Catherine Bruhier, Kim Renders, Genevieve Langlois, Pamela Matthews, and Karen Woolridge in the 1994 Grand Theatre production of "Flowers". Photo by Elisabeth Feryn.

Part One

Lights come up very slowly on a single, spacious, faintly rustic room that was once scrupulously clean but now bears the traces of disuse. One of the walls bears the remains of a small shrine, decayed but still ornate. Five little dressers, painted different colours are positioned downstage. Near the dressers are five small chairs emblazoned with different animal symbols. Everything in the room is marked by age.

SYLVIE stands alone in the room, looking around. She is in her late thirties. Her presence is febrile, electric; but she bears herself with an almost preternatural calm.

SYLVIE   Here. Back here. Such a long time. Dear God, help me. What am I doing back here. Back. One, two, three, four...You little fool, what can you possibly hope to accomplish? *(pulling a string of five paper dolls from her coat pocket)* Therese. Adele. Josee. Mariette...

Before she can say her own name, JOSEE and MARIETTE appear. SYLVIE quickly folds the dolls up and puts them in her pocket.

JOSEE   Sylvie! Thank God, you're here.

MARIETTE   Sylvie. Finally.

SYLVIE	Hello, Josee. Mariette...hi. I came as soon as I could.
JOSEE	We were so worried.
MARIETTE	We've been expecting you.
SYLVIE	I know. *(beat)* How is she?
MARIETTE	In and out of consciousness — she's having a hard time breathing. The doctor says she could go at any moment.
JOSEE	You should have come when I called. We've been here for days, Sylvie.
SYLVIE	I'm sorry, I told you, I —
JOSEE	What took you so long?
MARIETTE	She's been asking for you.
SYLVIE	For me?
JOSEE	Yes.
MARIETTE	Is that so strange?
SYLVIE	I think it's a little odd. I've stayed away — I haven't spoken to her in years. Now to be here again...it is strange. Don't you think?
MARIETTE	I think you should speak with her, now.
JOSEE	She's got something for you, Sylvie.
SYLVIE	What?
JOSEE	She keeps talking about a gift.
SYLVIE	What is it?
JOSEE	I don't know.
MARIETTE	There's only one way to find out.

SYLVIE	A gift. Now, of all times...what does she want from me?
JOSEE	No, Sylvie. She wants to give you something.
SYLVIE	It's a bit late for reparations.
MARIETTE	Maman never apologized for anything.
SYLVIE	Bribery, then. Well, I'm too old for candy. Alright! Here we are, we three, in this place. And I'm going to see Maman.
MARIETTE	Go on.
SYLVIE	Why should I go in there? Why should I do anything for her?
MARIETTE	There's no reason. Do it for yourself.
SYLVIE	Myself?
JOSEE	Do it for all of us, Sylvie.
SYLVIE	Alright. *(deciding to go)* One, two, three.
	Lights change as THERESE and ADELE appear.
THERESE	Four.
	The light flickers then goes out on THERESE.
ADELE	Five. *(holding up a little brown paper bag, and then, as MANON)* Sylvie, is that you?
SYLVIE	Maman.
ADELE	*(as MANON)* Take this.
SYLVIE	No.
ADELE	*(as MANON)* Take it.

SYLVIE	No, Maman, I don't want it.
ADELE	*(as MANON)* Take it as a token. A promise from mother to daughter.
THERESE	*(as ETIENNE)* In the names of Adele and Therese, take it.
SYLVIE	Don't you ever speak those names. Do you hear me? Don't speak them, don't think about them, don't think about us.
ADELE	*(as MANON)* Daughter, take this. Take it!
SYLVIE	No.
ADELE	*(as MANON)* Sylvie!

> *Lights change as the five women transform to little girls.*

JOSEE	Sylvie, hurry up!
MARIETTE	Come on, Sylvie, you slowpoke.
THERESE	Sylvie, Sylvie, get in here right now!
ADELE	Hurry up, Sylvie, or the Sandman's gonna get you.
CHORUS	Not the Sandman.
SYLVIE	I'm the Sandman! Wraaor! BOO!

> *As if in response to a command, they line up.*

SYLVIE	One.
MARIETTE	Two.
JOSEE	Three.
ADELE	Four.

THERESE   Five.

CHORUS   Matthew, Mark, Luke and John,
Bless the bed that I lay on.
Four corners to my bed,
Four angels 'round my head;
One to watch and one to pray,
And two to bear my soul away.

> *The girls stare down at their hands, speak as
> one, then break into different personas.*

CHORUS   *(awestruck)* Arms and legs the size of fingers.

ADELE   *(as MANON)* People will think we are pigs!

MARIETTE   *(as DRAPER)* I don't know if they're going to live,
we're taking it day by day.

SYLVIE   *(as a WASP)* Those filthy French papists should not
be allowed to breed so freely.

THERESE   *(as ETIENNE)* I don't know how this happened! I'm
the kind of guy they ought to put in jail.

JOSEE   *(as GLORIA SHERIDAN)* The Quints are a sign that
prosperity is finally on its way.

> *The girls transform back to themselves.*

SYLVIE   One!

MARIETTE   Two!

JOSEE   Three!

ADELE   Four!

THERESE   Five!

> *They wave to the audience then applaud.
> MARIETTE as DRAPER steps away from
> the group, speaking at a press conference.*

MARIETTE	*(as DRAPER)* In response to the increasing concern about the welfare of the Quintuplets, the Government of Ontario under the direction of Premier Hepburn has decided to build a Hospital to house the children away from the possibly septic conditions of the Paquette household. The Hospital will be built with funds raised through various commercial endorsements, and a special outdoor observation gallery will be attached which will allow the public to view the girls at play. The parents will be allowed visiting rights in accordance with sanitary procedures, but every aspect of the girls' upbringing will be monitored by myself as supervising physician and by a qualified nursing team. Our primary concern is that the Quints may continue to flourish through the application of modern medical care. *(pause)* We're all doing the best we can.

> *Applause. JOSEE transforms to NURSE, RACHEL WINTER, and blows a whistle.*

JOSEE	*(as NURSE)* Faced with the somewhat confusing task of treating — no, identifying these children as individuals in their own right, it becomes necessary to our mental health and their sense of security to assign certain identifying tags to their persons. A sort of visual key, if you will. Each child shall be treated with the unique attention necessary for the development of character and self. *(blowing whistle)* Fall in!

> *Each Quint moves to her downstage dresser and pulls a coloured hair ribbon, a stone, a stuffed animal, and a flower from the drawer. They attach the ribbons to their hair.*

SYLVIE	Sylvie Paquette. Colour: Blue. Stone: Lapis. Animal: Cat. Flower: Forget-me-not.
MARIETTE	Mariette Paquette. Colour: Red. Stone: Garnet. Animal: Raccoon. Flower: Daisy.
JOSEE	Josee Paquette. Colour: Yellow. Stone: Topaz. Animal: Teddy Bear. Flower: Trillium.

ADELE	Adele Paquette. Colour: Purple. Stone: Amethyst. Animal: Squirrel. Flower: Lily-of-the-valley.
THERESE	Therese Paquette. Colour: Green. Stone: Emerald. Animal: Robin. Flower: Queen Anne's lace.

The Quints join hands and group together.

CHORUS	We are all overly sensitive to change. You might even call us cowards.
MARIETTE	I suppose this is a result of all the years spent living in a hospital, among doctors and nurses who watched and regulated and charted the least anomaly or sign of indisposition.
CHORUS	It shows in peculiar ways, our antiseptic upbringing.
JOSEE	I, for instance, have the compulsion to brush my teeth after every meal and between times too. If I don't, I feel a sense of unease.
CHORUS	Unease.
SYLVIE	And perhaps, the careful washing of hands several times a day is the mark of a quintuplet.
CHORUS	Maman?
SYLVIE	She can watch us playing through the fence of the observation ground.

> *THERESE as ETIENNE addresses the audience. Music: "So Rare" by Guy Lombardo.*

THERESE	*(as ETIENNE)* Their mother misses them and so do I. Even though I'm just the father I often wonder if they don't miss us too I remember my own mother and I believe That nothing can take the place Of a mother's love and care.
SYLVIE	Squirrel!

Racing into a circle, ADELE leads a unison movement of smoothing dresses.

ADELE   One!

THERESE   Two!

JOSEE   Three!

MARIETTE   Four!

SYLVIE   Five!

ADELE   Raccoon!

They change positions, and MARIETTE leads them into a curtsey.

MARIETTE   One!

ADELE   Two!

SYLVIE   Three!

JOSEE   Four!

THERESE   Five!

MARIETTE   Teddy Bear!

They change positions once more and JOSEE leads them into a circle handclapping game. They count and clap simultaneously.

CHORUS   One! Two! Three! Four! Five!

JOSEE   Robin!

The others look to THERESE for leadership; she is staring out at the audience. The other girls follow her gaze and wave, in unison. The music fades. SYLVIE looks around.

SYLVIE	Twice a day we go outside to play in a big yard that has a large red fence around it. There's just the five of us, and two nurses, but I can hear things coming from that fence.
	The CHORUS mimics the voices of the tourists by mumbling and coughing.
SYLVIE	I know that there are people out there. Why can't I see them? Why don't the nurses notice? I have to find out who it is. I walk closer to the fence. I look up and wave. I hear the voices, I hear them! But Nursey comes and pulls me, pulls me away from the people.
CHORUS	*(as NURSE)* It's not nice to wave at the fence, Sylvie. It's not nice. Don't look at the silly fence. Come and play.
SYLVIE	But I heard them! The people! I can still hear them! Can't you hear?
CHORUS	*(as NURSE)* The Sandman is out there. Do you want to call the Sandman?
SYLVIE	No, no! I don't want to call the Sandman.
CHORUS	*(as NURSE)* Come along, Sylvie. Don't cry. You know what happens to little girls when they're bad and cry. There's a good girl.
SYLVIE	Must go play now. Must go play pretend.
CHORUS	*(as NURSE)* There's a good girl. Pretend.
THERESE	Robin!
	All the Quints run out, except for ADELE who takes their trademark chairs and begins arranging them on stage. THERESE joins her.
THERESE	Adele, what are you doing?

ADELE	Push the chairs around, out of order. Robin here, raccoon there, cat all the way around over here!
THERESE	Oh, that's bad. You're going to get in trouble.
ADELE	No, Therese. It's fun. Come on!
	MARIETTE and JOSEE come running in.
JOSEE	What are you doing, you two?
ADELE	Switch hair ribbons, quick!
	All the girls quickly trade hair ribbons, then sit, playing "musical chairs" to make sure they've got different identities. SYLVIE enters as a NURSE, pushing a trolley with four bowls and an identity chart on it.
SYLVIE	*(as NURSE)* Good morning, girls.
CHORUS	Good morning, Nurse.
	SYLVIE as NURSE hands out a bowl and spoon to each Quint. They each take one and answer, "Merci, mademoiselle." When they all have one, they mouth a grace, say "Amen," cross themselves and begin to eat.
SYLVIE	*(as NURSE)* How are we feeling today?
CHORUS	Fine, thank you.
SYLVIE	*(as NURSE)* I hope we're enjoying our oatmeal.
CHORUS	Oh yes, we certainly are.
	They kick at each other. ADELE flings a spoonful at JOSEE.
SYLVIE	*(as NURSE)* Mariette! What's got into you? You know better than to play with your food.

ADELE	But I didn't.
SYLVIE	*(as NURSE)* I saw you throw it.
ADELE	But I'm Adele, can't you tell?
SYLVIE	*(as NURSE)* No, you're Mariette. *(referring to chart)* You're wearing the red ribbon.
ADELE	You'll have to look closer than that.
SYLVIE	*(as NURSE)* Fine. Now just eat your breakfast in peace.

> *They resume eating. JOSEE throws a well-aimed spoonful at MARIETTE's forehead.*

SYLVIE	*(as NURSE)* Therese, stop that right now.
THERESE	I didn't do anything!
SYLVIE	*(as NURSE)* I'm not speaking to you, Josee. Therese, you just threw that porridge at your sister. Adele, cut it out!
THERESE	I didn't do anything.
ADELE	Me either.

> *SYLVIE refers to the chart.*

SYLVIE	*(as NURSE)* You're Therese, you have the green ribbon and the robin chair.
JOSEE	No, I'm Josee, I have the yellow ribbon—
MARIETTE	And I have the Teddy Bear chair!
SYLVIE	*(as NURSE)* What's going on here? What have you done?
ADELE	We changed everything around!

> *They pull their ribbons off and replace them with the right ones, forming a circle around NURSE, clanking spoons on bowls.*

JOSEE   Now, can you tell us apart?

> *They start to dance a ring around her, chanting.*

CHORUS   *(severally)* Who am I? Who am I? Who am I?

SYLVIE   *(as NURSE)* Stop that! Therese!

CHORUS   Oui?

SYLVIE   *(as NURSE)* Adele! Come here right now!

CHORUS   Oui?

SYLVIE   *(as NURSE)* Josee! Mariette! Sylvie!

CHORUS   Oui? Oui? Oui? Oui? Oui?

SYLVIE   *(as NURSE)* That's enough! Stop it! Please please stop it! Stop it right now!

> *She bursts into tears and stamps her foot. They break the circle and comfort her.*

MARIETTE   It's okay, Nursey. Come here. Sit down and learn about the five little pigs.

JOSEE   One little pig went to market.

THERESE   One little pig stayed home.

ADELE   One little pig ate roast beef.

SYLVIE   *(as SYLVIE)* One little pig had none.

MARIETTE   But five little pigs said...

CHORUS   Oui! Oui! Oui! Oui! Oui!

ADELE   All the way home!

> *ADELE transforms to MANON and steps
> forward. SYLVIE sits with the others behind
> her, cutting out a string of paper dolls. At
> the appropriate moment, she softly echoes,
> "who said that?"*

ADELE   *(as MANON)* The situation has become intolerable
for the girls and for their father and myself, as these
medical people teach the girls to love only them and
to hate their real parents. The nurses are barely polite
when Etienne and I visit and rude when we leave. I
can hear them snickering. Let me tell you: just the
other day I went to visit, and kissed all the girls
goodbye. Therese, that the others call Peewee, said,
"Another kiss, Maman," and embraced me again.
Then all the girls said, "Another kiss, Maman," and
they were really happy to get kisses. Then that nurse,
Mrs. Winter, came in and said, "Who said that? Who
wanted another kiss?" She was very threatening, and
the Quints were really afraid, I can tell you. "Tell
me!" she said again. So, little Sylvie put her chin up
and said, "It was all of us, Nurse. We all wanted
another kiss." "If I ever hear you say that again,"
Mrs. Winter said, "you know what will happen to
you." Oh, she's a real devil, I tell you. And this is
only one example of her cruelty. I am convinced that
she is planting a seed of death in the little ones' hearts
as she teaches them to hate their mother. I appeal to
your great heart and to the love you have for your
family, Monsieur Armstrong, when I ask you as a
guardian of my daughters to get rid of this woman. If
I can't have my girls in my own home, then I insist
that they grow in a normal environment.

Respectfully yours,
Mme. Manon Paquette.
15 August, 1939

> *SYLVIE remains seated. She holds out the
> paper dolls to her mother. ADELE as
> MANON takes the dolls, then pulls a paper
> bag from her jacket and offers SYLVIE a
> candy from it. JOSEE as GLORIA
> SHERIDAN looks on. THERESE
> transforms to NURSE and exits with the
> breakfast tray. MARIETTE transforms to
> DR. DRAPER, and turns on MANON.*

MARIETTE   *(as DRAPER)* What are you doing here? This is not your day to visit. I must ask you to let that child go and leave immediately.

ADELE   *(as MANON)* You see the way I am treated? I'm not even allowed to visit my daughters. Come here, Sylvie.

MARIETTE   *(as DRAPER)* Who is this?

JOSEE   *(as GLORIA, extending her hand)* Gloria Sheridan, *Toronto Telegram*. And you—?

MARIETTE   *(as DRAPER)* Draper. Dr. John Draper. Excuse me, Miss. Look, Mme. Paquette, I'm sick to death of listening to your ranting and raving. You're wasting my time, you're wasting Miss Sheridan's time, and Sylvie should be having her nap.

ADELE   *(as MANON)* You hear that? *(grabbing SYLVIE)* I'm not leaving until I am heard.

JOSEE   *(as GLORIA, to DRAPER)* Look, if there's a better time, I can return.

MARIETTE   *(as DRAPER)* No, no. Mme. Paquette, if you have something to say, then by all means, say it.

ADELE   *(as MANON, to GLORIA)* Are you taking this down?

JOSEE   *(as GLORIA)* Yes, Mme. Paquette.

ADELE   (*as MANON*) Good. *(beat)* I wish to tell everyone in
             Canada that the people running this hospital are
             mistreating my children.

MARIETTE   (*as DRAPER*) Preposterous. This is a modern facility
             with trained staff. No children receive more diligent
             care.

ADELE   (*as MANON*) They should be at home with their
             father and me.

MARIETTE   (*as DRAPER*) That is a guardianship issue. It has
             nothing to do with me. Address your criticisms to the
             politicians and let me get on with my work.

                     THERESE as DR. BARKER enters,
                     fumbling with a film camera and tripod.

THERESE   (*as BARKER*) John, can you give me a hand with
             this blasted thing? *(noticing SYLVIE)* Hello there,
             little girl.

SYLVIE   Hello.

ADELE   (*as MANON, to SYLVIE*) Shush, you. (*to
             DRAPER*) Who is that?

MARIETTE   (*as DRAPER*) This is Dr. Barker, the eminent child
             psychologist from Toronto. He's going to be
             conducting some studies.

THERESE   (*as BARKER*) Passive experimentation.

MARIETTE   (*as DRAPER*) Doctor, this is Mme. Manon
             Paquette.

THERESE   (*as BARKER*) Ah, yes, the mother.

ADELE   (*as MANON*) Yes, the mother!

JOSEE   (*as GLORIA*) Gloria Sheridan, the *Telegram*.

THERESE   (*as BARKER*) Is something wrong?

JOSEE   *(as GLORIA)* Mme. Paquette has some questions about the quality of care here.

THERESE   *(as BARKER)* That's only natural. What are the questions?

ADELE   *(as MANON)* My children are malnourished. They are starved in their bodies and hungry for the care and love that only a real family can give.

THERESE   *(as BARKER)* These are serious allegations.

ADELE   *(as MANON)* All you have to do is look at them to see my point.

                     SYLVIE has moved over to where BARKER left the camera: she is playing with it.

THERESE   *(as BARKER)* Mme. Paquette, your children are receiving all the benefits of a modern medical upbringing. No, little girl, don't touch that. They're surrounded by a loving staff who monitor every aspect of their nurturing. Sylvie, no. A sort of surrogate family. *(taking the camera from SYLVIE)* Give me that.

ADELE   *(as MANON)* They don't look like healthy children. Get up, Sylvie. Look. They are too thin! It's not normal, they should be chubbier.

MARIETTE   *(as DRAPER)* We keep their weight down to strengthen their resistance to disease. *(to MANON)* As I've explained to you *ad nauseum.*

                     DRAPER places his hands on SYLVIE's shoulders.

JOSEE   *(as GLORIA)* Mme. Paquette, what do you have to say to this? We need evidence.

ADELE   *(as MANON)* I am their mother, and I know what's best for them. I know how to raise children. I already have five at home. The women of Canada will know what I'm talking about.

MARIETTE	*(as DRAPER)* I don't mean to offend you, Mme. Paquette, but those other children of yours are not the same as these girls.
ADELE	*(as MANON)* Children are children. Sylvie, come here. Come to Maman.

SYLVIE sits still.

JOSEE	*(as GLORIA)* Dr. Barker, what exactly are you planning to study and how will you go about it?
THERESE	*(as BARKER)* I'm trying to determine if identity influences behaviour. You see, we're looking down the road for these girls. We're trying to create the optimum circumstances for them later on in life. *(looking at SYLVIE through the camera then walking backwards, while she follows him, looking into the lens)* It involves special treatment that they simply couldn't get at home, no matter how devoted the mother.
JOSEE	*(as GLORIA)* What about the lack of emotional stimulation?
MARIETTE	*(as DRAPER)* There is no lack of anything here. Sylvie. Sylvie, come to Doctor.
SYLVIE	Doctor, doctor!

SYLVIE throws her arms around DRAPER and starts rooting through his pockets.

ADELE	*(as MANON)* Sylvie, it's Maman. Sylvie. Sylvie, come here!
MARIETTE	*(as DRAPER)* Sylvie, go see your mother.

SYLVIE goes to MANON.

SYLVIE	Maman. When are you coming to visit again?
ADELE	*(as MANON)* Sylvie.

MARIETTE	*(as DRAPER)* Do you see a problem here? No. You can't own the children's affections, Madame. There is more than enough to spread around.
JOSEE	*(as GLORIA)* Do you love your Maman, Sylvie?
SYLVIE	I love Maman. I love Doctor. I want to play with Doctor.
	SYLVIE pulls away from MANON.
ADELE	*(as MANON)* Sylvie, Sylvie!
	Light change. The girls transform back to themselves.
THERESE	Sylvie! Sylvie, hurry up!
MARIETTE	Come on, Sylvie, you slowpoke.
ADELE	Sylvie, get in here right now.
JOSEE	Hurry up, Sylvie, or the Sandman's gonna get you.
CHORUS	Not the Sandman!
SYLVIE	I'm the Sandman. Booo!
	The Quints each step into a spotlight and point up. They are outside, in the observation ground.
SYLVIE	I climb to the top of the swing-set. I hear a sound like the fans in our room at night, but I know it's not that. Do you know what it is? It's a secret. It's the voices out there, it's a hundred gasps.
CHORUS	A hundred gasps.
ADELE	What can I do? Anything you want. I hold onto the bar with my hands, and pull my legs up over my head. A somersault. I pull my knees over and ankles up, lock knees over bar and hang upside down like a bat.

THERESE	Put my hands on the bar and pull myself up, straight like a tin soldier. Balance on the bar...
CHORUS	...Carefully, easy now...
THERESE	...pull legs and ankles higher and grasp. Stand and walk it like a cat...teeter-totter.
CHORUS	Teeter-totter, a hundred gasps, they are looking at me!

> *Quint CHORUS transforms into NURSE voice.*

CHORUS	*(as NURSE)* Play time over, play time up. Time to go in, get down from the bar.
MARIETTE	I can do anything. I am the Queen. Walk back and forth, wave, curtsey, bow. Time to go in? Queen of the castle, how do I get down?
CHORUS	*(as NURSE)* Get down, grab my arm, you'll fall down.
MARIETTE	No, I won't. I stand, considering.
JOSEE	Bend over slowly, grab the bar, balanced bum in the air. Bend knees, put one foot over, two feet over, sitting now. Swing backwards, pull knees to face and under bar, hanging body stretched out below. Hold a second, then drop.
CHORUS	*(as NURSE)* Show off, show off. Get inside!
SYLVIE	Dust off my bum, wave once, skip back in.

> *SYLVIE brushes off her behind, waves at the audience. The other girls hurry to their dressers and put on short white gloves.*

ADELE	Hurry up, Sylvie, or the Sandman will get you.
MARIETTE	Mind your own business, Adele, or the Sandman will get *you*.

JOSEE   Stop mouthing off, Mariette, or the Sandman is gonna come.

THERESE   You girls all better do as you're told, or I'll get the Sandman.

SYLVIE   You know where the Sandman lives. You know where the Sandman breathes. You know where he's waiting. In the Quiet Room.

CHORUS   The Quiet Room —

SYLVIE   Where mouthy little, bossy little, grumpy little quintuplets go.

CHORUS   *(coy)* The bad girls.

> *They wave shyly, then regally, and curtsey to the audience. A microphone lowers from the ceiling. THERESE walks to the microphone, and ADELE follows, leading SYLVIE, MARIETTE and JOSEE.*
>
> *Bright lights. A live-to-air studio at the Canadian Broadcasting Corporation. THERESE as HOST, ADELE as MANON. She holds a paper bag and distributes candies to the girls.*

THERESE   *(as HOST)* Alright. Before we go on the air, I just want to make sure that we all know what we're doing. Now girls, what are you going to say?

SYLVIE   We're going to say, "Happy Mother's Day," and then sing, "There'll Always Be An England." Then we ask the people to come and visit us in the playground.

THERESE   *(as HOST)* That's right. Very good. Are you ready?

CHORUS   Yes.

ADELE   *(as MANON)* Now girls, do as you were told.

VOICEOVER	Five seconds to air... 3, 2,1.

On-air light. Signature music: "Vieni, vieni" by Rudy Vallee, fades as THERESE speaks.

THERESE — *(as HOST)* Welcome to the Mother's Day, 1941 edition of "Your Best Bet." Today we have an extra special treat for our listeners, as Canada's own Paquette Quintuplets are here in the studio with us. Yes, right here. And they're anxious to say hello to everyone out there in Radioland. Isn't that right, girls? *(pause)* Girls? *(pause)* Well, heh-heh, they must be feeling a bit shy. We'll speak with them in a moment. But right now, here's Miss Vera Lynn with the number one song on today's hit parade.

Music: "There'll be Bluebirds over theWhite Cliffs of Dover." On-air light goes off.

THERESE — *(as HOST)* Alright. What's the problem?

ADELE — *(as MANON)* Oh dear, I don't know. They did it so well at the rehearsal.

THERESE — *(as HOST)* Cat got your tongue, girls? *(pause)* Look, Mme. Paquette, we're running out of time and this is live to air. Can't you do something?

ADELE — *(as MANON)* What should I do?

THERESE — *(as HOST)* Speak to them. You're their mother.

ADELE — *(as MANON)* Girls, I want you to do just as you were told.

SYLVIE — We are, Maman. You said, no talking on the radio. It's dirty.

THERESE — *(as HOST)* What the hell's going on here? What are we going to do now? Come on, Quints. When that red light comes on, speak into the microphone.

JOSEE — No, no. It's dirty!

THERESE   *(as HOST)* There's got to be something—

> *THERESE, as HOST, gets down on all fours and brays like a donkey. SYLVIE, MARIETTE and JOSEE start to laugh.*

VOICEOVER   5 seconds to air...3, 2, 1.

MARIETTE   You're funny.

ADELE   *(as MANON)* Shhh!

> *On-air light. Music fades slowly.*

THERESE   *(as HOST)* And, welcome back to "Your Best Bet." For those of you just tuning in, I want to say that we've got the five most famous little ladies in the world right here in the studio, and they want to speak to you. Girls, say hello to all the people out there.

> *Pause. THERESE mimes the donkey braying. MARIETTE, SYLVIE and JOSEE suppress giggles. Dead air.*

THERESE   *(as HOST)* Ah-hah. Well, now —

ADELE   *(as MANON)* I can speak.

THERESE   *(as HOST)* Oh, that's right! Ladies and gentlemen, and all you mothers out there, this is Mme. Paquette—

ADELE   *(as MANON)* Manon.

THERESE   *(as HOST)* Manon Paquette. It's especially appropriate that she be here with us today, since she is the mother of these wonderful children.

ADELE   *(as MANON)* That's right. Hello? I just want to say that it will only be a real Mother's Day for me when I can finally have my darling daughters at home with their father and me. I know that all the mothers out there must share my pain and grief at my outcast state, for it's been seven years now that they've been away from their home.

THERESE	*(as HOST)* Ah, that's wonderful, Mme. Paquette. Maybe we can talk about this later...but now for a musical interlude.
	Music: Tommy Dorsey's "You Must Have Been a Beautiful Baby." On-air light goes off.
THERESE	*(as HOST)* What's going on here? You're ruining this broadcast.
ADELE	*(as MANON)* I can speak my peace and the Quints will sing; or, if I can't, they won't make a peep. And that is that.
THERESE	*(as HOST)* But that's blackmail! Jesus Murphy, lady, there's a war going on. The public wants to hear something that will make them feel good.
ADELE	*(as MANON)* Then they will have to hear it from you.
THERESE	*(as HOST)* What do the girls want to do?
ADELE	*(as MANON)* They do as I tell them. *(handing out candy)* Isn't that right, Sylvie?
SYLVIE	Yes, Maman.
MARIETTE	I want to sing, "Frère Jacques."
ADELE	*(as MANON)* You'll do as I say.
VOICEOVER	5 seconds to air... 3, 2, 1.
	On-air light. Music fades.
THERESE	*(as HOST)* Welcome back, listeners. Before we broke, we were listening to Manon Paquette telling us about her experiences as mother of the Quintuplets.
MARIETTE	Can I sing it now?
THERESE	*(as HOST)* By all means, Quin, go ahead.

MARIETTE   Maman?

ADELE   *(as MANON)* Yes, Mariette, you may sing.

MARIETTE   *(singing)* Frère Jacques, Frère Jacques
Dormez-vous? Dormez-vous?

CHORUS   Sonnez le matin, sonnez le matin
Din dan don. Din dan don.

> *MARIETTE, JOSEE and SYLVIE continue
> song as underscore.*

THERESE   *(as HOST)* Thank you girls! And now, we'll be going
into our next item—

> *When ADELE breaks in, THERESE
> transforms to Quint and joins in the song.*

ADELE   *(as MANON)* I just want to say that I am very sorry
the war is on in Europe, and I know that many
women are missing their sons. But here in Canada,
there are battles that I must fight as long as Etienne
and I are forced to live without our babies. Is that
right? Is that just? Thank you.

> *ADELE joins in the song.*

JOSEE   Bye-bye! Happy Mother's Day! Come visit us this
summer!

CHORUS   Din dan don.
DIN DAN DON.

> *All five girls bunch together and hold their
> left wrists with their right hands. Heads
> bowed, they shyly sing.*

CHORUS   "There'll always be an England
And England shall be free
If England means as much to you
As England means to me."

> *SYLVIE breaks from the line and comes forward, removing her white gloves. MARIETTE transforms to DRAPER; JOSEE, ADELE and THERESE to NURSES. MARIETTE steps forward to SYLVIE.*

MARIETTE   *(as DRAPER)* Come here, girlies. I want to see my girls.

SYLVIE   No. We want Maman.

ADELE   *(as NURSE 1)* Maman is not here right now.

JOSEE   *(as NURSE 2)* Go on, say hello to Doctor.

SYLVIE   No! We don't like Doctor. He's dirty.

ADELE   *(as NURSE 1)* Now wherever did you hear a thing like that?

MARIETTE   *(as DRAPER)* Three guesses and the first two don't count.

THERESE   *(as NURSE 3)* Now girls. Why don't you like the Doctor?

SYLVIE   Because he is the Devil.

THERESE   *(as NURSE 3)* Don't you ever say a thing like that!

SYLVIE   We want our Maman.

JOSEE   *(as NURSE 2)* I don't understand what's come over them. *(approaching SYLVIE)* What's the matter?

> *SYLVIE frantically digs in her pocket and, finding a candy, pops it in her mouth. The others watch, horrified.*

MARIETTE   *(as DRAPER)* What is that?

ADELE   *(as NURSE 1)* It looks like a candy.

THERESE   *(as NURSE 3)* Oh my God, that's a candy.

JOSEE   Is that candy, Sylvie?

SYLVIE   *(sucking away intently)* Maman always gives us candy.

MARIETTE   *(as DRAPER)* Ah. Now I understand. Nurse? *(the 3 NURSES snap to attention)* You know I forbade sweets in this Nursery.

THERESE   *(as NURSE 3)* It's not my fault, Doctor.

JOSEE   *(as NURSE 2)* Doctor, I didn't know they had it.

ADELE   *(as NURSE 1)* It must have been sneaked in.

MARIETTE   *(as DRAPER)* You watch those people when they come to visit. You know how sly they are.

NURSES 1, 2 & 3   Yes, Sir!

> *DRAPER approaches SYLVIE.*

MARIETTE   *(as DRAPER)* Now girlie, give it over.

SYLVIE   No.

MARIETTE   *(as DRAPER)* Give me that candy.

SYLVIE   No.

MARIETTE   *(as DRAPER)* Open your mouth.

SYLVIE   No.

> *NURSES 1 and 3 hold SYLVIE's hands behind her back. NURSE 2 puts a hand on SYLVIE's lower jaw and shakes it. SYLVIE spits the candy out. The NURSES draw back.*

MARIETTE	*(as DRAPER, to NURSES)* Now, now. Calm down. It's all over. *(to SYLVIE)* Don't you know that sweets are bad for you? Come here.
SYLVIE	No. Devil. You're the Devil. Maman says so. We hate you.
MARIETTE	*(as DRAPER)* Put her in the Quiet Room.
SYLVIE	No. No!
JOSEE	*(as NURSE 2)* That's enough. Sylvie, come on now.
SYLVIE	No. Maman! Maman!

> *JOSEE leads SYLVIE, followed by ADELE and THERESE, slightly away from DRAPER. They freeze in tableau; JOSEE with SYLVIE, ADELE and THERESE as parents and MARIETTE as DRAPER looking at SYLVIE.*

JOSEE	*(as NURSE 2)* Dr. Draper permits the parents to see the babies occasionally, but due to the extreme care required, neither Mr. or Mrs. Paquette handle the Quintuplets. They are left in the hands of the good doctor, who has brought more than 1700 babies into this world, and loves them all.

> *JOSEE, ADELE AND THERESE remove their gloves. MARIETTE removes her gloves during the following speech.*

MARIETTE	*(as DRAPER)* The Paquettes have finally won their custody battle, so it seems my usefulness is at an end. I hope the girls make an easy switch from Hospital to Home, that it is possible to trade in one set of caretakers for another. I know that I speak for the entire medical team when I say how much we will all miss the Quints. It's as if they were my own...*(beat)* Were we right to take these children? For whatever reasons? Only time will tell. *(beat)* Happy birthday and good luck, girls. I hope for your continued health and happiness.

*Transformation to Quints. Outside the
nursery, 1942.*

JOSEE   Mariette and Adele are so lucky. Look. Their colours
are in the beautiful sunset.

MARIETTE   But Josee, your colour is in the sunshine.

ADELE   And Sylvie's is the big blue sky.

THERESE   Where's mine? I can't see it at all.

MARIETTE   It's underneath the snow, Therese.

SYLVIE   Yes, Therese. When the snow melts, your colour will
be all over the land.

JOSEE   You'll be luckiest of all.

THERESE   But when will the snow melt? Please tell me,
Sylvie. You know about everything.

SYLVIE   Soon, Therese. In the springtime when everything is
alive and growing. When the new house is built and
we move into it.

THERESE   But I don't want to leave the Hospital. I want to stay
with the Nurses. I like it here.

SYLVIE   It's going to be a giant house for us to play in. With
the whole family. That's why it's called the Big
House. Maman said we'll be free when we move
there.

JOSEE   Is that when all the people will come back?

ADELE   Yes, Sylvie, where have the people gone?

SYLVIE   They've all gone away to the war.

MARIETTE   To war, to war, they've gone away to war...

JOSEE   Now there's nobody to play for.

SYLVIE	I guess we'll have to play for ourselves.
MARIETTE	To war, to war, they've gone away to war...
THERESE	And they don't care about us any more.
MARIETTE	That's good, Therese. "To war, to war, they've gone away to war And they don't care about us any more."

> *CHORUS joins in singing this refrain.*

CHORUS	"To war, to war, they've gone away to war And they don't care about us any more."

> *Pause. Sunset light deepens. Music:*
> *"Perfidia" by Glenn Miller. The big house,*
> *1946. Transition to adolescence. In unison,*
> *the girls' focus changes: they pick up the*
> *flowers from their dressers and pose with*
> *them, pirouette, curtsey. During SYLVIE's*
> *speech they remove their hair bows and hold*
> *them. SYLVIE turns to the audience.*

SYLVIE I must take care. Do you know what that means? It does not mean being careful. It means that I got lucky. I am the oldest and the smartest. That's what they tell me, my sisters. And so, I take care of them. They are as children to me. We are bound together in ways you couldn't even dream of, we five. So, you can't understand this thing. Nobody can. I watch over them, I guard the bond that protects us. They are me and I am them.

> *All the girls look up. Although they speak*
> *in unison, each one has her own 'take' on the*
> *next speech:*

CHORUS It's just that sometimes I would like to take my money, and I don't know, go somewhere. The Caribbean, perhaps. And drink piña coladas, and sleep on the beach, and be me, and nobody else.

	During the following, they carefully pocket their hairbows.
SYLVIE	But that's not the way it is. And so, I stand or fall by my sisters. I watch over them. I am taking care.
	All five salute smartly. *The big house, 1946. JOSEE comes* *forward. The other girls stay in unison.*
JOSEE	It is morning. The others have gone down to breakfast and I will be late. Mustn't be late!
CHORUS	Pappa doesn't like it.
JOSEE	I hurry to get dressed. But nothing goes right today. I couldn't make the bed without lumps, then I upset the water glass, and now it seems that I must change my panties. I pull down my stockings and then my pants.
CHORUS	What's this? What have I done?
JOSEE	I don't remember hurting myself.
CHORUS	Red stain spreading.
JOSEE	A red stain spreading. It smells flat.
CHORUS	What have I done? What can I do?
JOSEE	I can't tell Maman. She'll think I've been touching myself. What will I do? I must get to breakfast. I put on three pairs of panties and creep downstairs. But I can't hide my shame. I'm so scared.
CHORUS	I'm so afraid —
JOSEE	I can't eat. Pappa sends me away from the table. Then Maman sees my behind and yells at me. Everyone turns around to watch as I leave the room.
CHORUS	I have never felt so dirty and ashamed.

JOSEE	And alone as I do right now. Then my brother wants to pull down all our pants to see — and suddenly I'm relieved. I take refuge...

The others join JOSEE.

CHORUS	Refuge...
JOSEE	...in the fiveness of my being.

Stillness. The beat is broken when MARIETTE, JOSEE, ADELE and THERESE turn on SYLVIE, yelling:

CHORUS	I see England I see France I see Sylvie's underpants!

MARIETTE, ADELE, and THERESE exit leaving SYLVIE and JOSEE alone. JOSEE transforms to a brother, GASTON.

SYLVIE	Get out of my room, Gaston. Get out!
JOSEE	*(as GASTON)* Watcha gonna do, make me?
SYLVIE	Yes.
JOSEE	*(as GASTON)* Oh, yeah. Just try it skinny. Besides, it's not just your room. It's everybody's. Pappa says so, so you'd better share it, or else. You're not in the Nursery now!
SYLVIE	Please leave me alone.
JOSEE	*(as GASTON)* You're so stuck up. You think you're so special. Freak.
SYLVIE	At least I'm not ugly and stupid like you.
JOSEE	*(as GASTON)* You're the ugly one. You're five ugly rats. Why don't you just get out of here? I wish you'd just die and leave us alone.
SYLVIE	Shut up.

JOSEE	*(as GASTON)* Everything was better before you came along. Everyone says so. Even Mamam says so.
SYLVIE	That's not true. Shut up.

MARIETTE enters on GASTON's line.

MARIETTE	What's going on? Sylvie, what's he doing to you?
JOSEE	*(as GASTON)* I was just telling her that Maman wishes you'd never been born.
MARIETTE	Maman is a fat ugly pig.
SYLVIE	Mariette!
JOSEE	*(as GASTON)* I'm telling Pappa you said that.
MARIETTE	I don't care what you tell him, stupid. Say whatever you like. You lie about us all the time, anyway.
JOSEE	*(as GASTON)* I am, I'm telling. And you know what else? Maman was skinny before she had you. It was you freaks that made her fat.
SYLVIE	We did not.
MARIETTE	That's not true.

ADELE and THERESE enter during GASTON's line.

JOSEE	*(as GASTON)* Did so. Just ask her. And I'm telling. Pappa! Oh, you're really gonna get it now. Pappa!

ADELE and THERESE's lines run right on each other.

ADELE	What's the matter, Sylvie?
THERESE	Mariette, what's wrong?
JOSEE	*(as GASTON)* She's gonna get the strap. Pappa!

> *JOSEE goes to the door as GASTON and*
> *freezes. Pause. JOSEE transforms to Quint.*

MARIETTE   I hate this place. I hate it! I'm going to run away.

THERESE   How do you do that?

MARIETTE   It's simple. You just get your things and go.

ADELE   How do you know that?

MARIETTE   I read it in a book. Come on. Let's get our clothes and go!

JOSEE   But how do we get past the dogs and the fence?

MARIETTE   I don't know.

SYLVIE   Forget it, Mariette. There's no way we can go.

ADELE   Maybe if we pray very hard, God will help us.

> *Pause. They look at ADELE, then kneel.*

JOSEE   God, we know you don't have time for silly girls.

THERESE   But maybe you could listen to us right now.

SYLVIE   Sweet Jesus, deliver us in our time of need.

ADELE   Save us from the devils in our life.

MARIETTE   Or just strike our enemies dead as soon as you can.

CHORUS   Amen. *(making the sign of the cross)*

> *ADELE begins to sing chorus from "Kyrie*
> *Eleison," joined by the others. She walks*
> *over to her shrine. ADELE's room, the big*
> *house, 1947. ADELE alone at her shrine.*

ADELE   *(singing)* Kyrie Eleison

SYLVIE   What are you doing, Adele?

ADELE puts her hand over her heart.

ADELE Oh, Sylvie. You startled me.

SYLVIE Sorry. *(pause)* What's that?

ADELE It's a shrine. I made it myself.

SYLVIE A shrine...who's it to?

ADELE Frère André.

SYLVIE But he's not a saint. Why don't you make it to Saint Joseph?

ADELE Frère André may not be a saint yet, but he will be canonized. I know it. He performed the three miracles; it's just a matter of time. Look. I have a crucifix here, and there's Saint Joseph with The Baby and The Blessed Virgin.

SYLVIE looks at the figurines.

SYLVIE Where did you get these figures? Adele? You didn't take them from the Crêche.

ADELE It's only March. No one will know. I'll put them back, Sylvie, I promise. Before Advent.

SYLVIE What if Maman sees them here? You know how she feels about that Crêche.

ADELE It's better that I have them. They'll just sit in the cellar all year long.

SYLVIE You'd better keep your shrine hidden. She'll kill you if she finds them.

ADELE No, I believe she would understand.

SYLVIE Adele, you are so good. *(touching ADELE's cheek)* What's that, there?

ADELE That — that is the sacred heart of Frère André.

SYLVIE   What?

ADELE   Well, no. It's not his real heart. That's in
             Montreal in the basilica. But I needed a relic. So I
             soaked some cotton batting in some blood and put it
             in the jar. With the candlelight, it looks real enough.

SYLVIE   You did that.

ADELE   It makes it real, Sylvie. You have to make a
             sacrifice.

SYLVIE   Adele, have you been mortifying yourself?

ADELE   Don't tell. It's just a little blood. It's good for me. It
             relieves the pressure in here. *(indicating her head)*
             This shrine is my refuge. My sanctuary. When I look
             on it and pray, I leave the world behind.

             SYLVIE holds the little jar to the light.

SYLVIE   A living Saint who has a heart more precious than
             the foreskin of Christ.

ADELE   Yes, that's what they say. *(beat)* What's a
             foreskin?

SYLVIE   I don't know.

             SYLVIE puts the jar back in its niche.
             ADELE transforms to MANON.

SYLVIE   Maman, what's a foreskin?

ADELE   *(as MANON)* What?

SYLVIE   A foreskin. What is it?

ADELE   *(as MANON)* Nothing that you need to worry about.
             Where did you hear that word?

SYLVIE	Frère André. It's what they say about him. "A living Saint who has a heart more precious than the foreskin of Christ." What does it mean?
ADELE	*(as MANON)* Come here. *(pause)* Sylvie, do you know what a...penis...is?
SYLVIE	Yes.
ADELE	*(as MANON)* How do you know that?
SYLVIE	I have brothers.
ADELE	*(as MANON)* Some boys do not have these little pieces of skin on their ah...Well. It is removed after they are born. It's not clean. Do you understand?
SYLVIE	But then, why do they say that about Jesus?
ADELE	*(as MANON)* Don't you ever say that about your Lord! It is a desecration of the Holy Mystery.
SYLVIE	I only wanted to know.
ADELE	*(as MANON)* Look, Sylvie. I will say this once, then I don't want to hear any more about it. You don't need to know about such things. You will never have to deal with that part of life. It's not for you. You will not date boys, you will never fall in love, you won't get married and you will never bear children.
SYLVIE	Why not?
ADELE	*(as MANON)* Because you're special. You're different from all that business. That is not why God sent you to this earth. You will stay here, you five, and live with your father and me. And we will protect you from that part of life. Do you understand?
SYLVIE	Yes, Maman.
	Light change. ADELE transforms to Quint.
ADELE	What is a foreskin, Sylvie?

SYLVIE   I don't know — it's just something to do with boys, Adele. It's not important for us to know about it.

ADELE   It must be very special if it has to do with Jesus.

SYLVIE   It's part of the Holy Mystery. That's all I know. And that we must never, ever, come into contact with it.

ADELE   Well, I have the heart here. I don't suppose I need the foreskin too.

SYLVIE   That's right.

ADELE   Are you alright, Sylvie?

SYLVIE   Yes, I'm fine.

ADELE   Good. Because we love you so very, very much.

           ADELE hugs SYLVIE, who hugs her back. They laugh. Music: "There, I've Said It Again" by Vaughan Monroe, comes over the radio. SYLVIE and ADELE are joined by JOSEE, MARIETTE and THERESE. SYLVIE sits down with a sketch book and begins to draw her sisters. JOSEE addresses MARIETTE.

JOSEE   First, I come up to you. We look at each other. You're supposed to blush. I say, "Excuse me, Miss. Would you do me the honour?" I bow. You stand up and curtsey.

MARIETTE   Well, that part is easy enough.

SYLVIE   Alright, so do it. *(indicating THERESE and ADELE)* You two, as well.

           JOSEE approaches MARIETTE. THERESE approaches ADELE.

JOSEE   Excuse me, Miss. Would you do me the honour?

MARIETTE   Why, certainly, Sir.

THERESE	Do me the honour, Miss?
ADELE	Alright.
JOSEE	Now, I put my left hand on your back, and you put this hand here. That's right, Therese. Now take my other hand.
ADELE	This feels silly.
MARIETTE	It's stupid.
JOSEE	Just do it. Come on.
MARIETTE	No.
SYLVIE	Come on. Don't be a spoilsport, Mariette. Therese, Adele, get up and dance!
MARIETTE	Why don't you do it, if you're so eager?
SYLVIE	Because I'm the Court Artist. *(beat, MARIETTE laughs)* Besides, Josee knows more about it.
JOSEE	Now. I'm going to lead with my right foot here.
SYLVIE	Pay attention, Therese!
JOSEE	And your foot follows it. Then the other one. That's it.

They dance, after a fashion.

SYLVIE	It looks good. How does it feel?
MARIETTE	It feels goofy.
JOSEE	It's supposed to feel romantic. You're supposed to be transported by romance. The moon is reflecting off the water, it catches the gleam in your eye — like so…
THERESE	Then what?

JOSEE	You surrender to the romance of it all.
ADELE	What does that mean?
JOSEE	It means you give in —
MARIETTE	It means you kiss him.
THERESE	Kiss?
ADELE	Kiss?
SYLVIE	Kiss?
JOSEE	Yes.
ADELE	Oh God.
JOSEE	Switch!

THERESE grabs SYLVIE's sketch pad.

| THERESE | Your turn, Sylvie. |
| SYLVIE | No. |

MARIETTE grabs SYLVIE's arm and pulls her up.

| MARIETTE | Stop watching everybody else. Get up and do it yourself. |

They resume dancing. This time SYLVIE and MARIETTE are partnered, as are ADELE and JOSEE. THERESE looks on, laughing.

JOSEE	Now the moonlight, in the eyes —
MARIETTE	It's blinding me, I can't see!
JOSEE	Shut up. And the kiss. *(dipping ADELE and pecking her cheek)*

ADELE	Blech!
	MARIETTE and SYLVIE kiss. The girls all burst out laughing. THERESE transforms to ETIENNE.
THERESE	*(as ETIENNE)* What's going on here?
SYLVIE	We're just playing.
THERESE	*(as ETIENNE)* Playing at what?
SYLVIE	Listening to the music.
THERESE	*(as ETIENNE)* Turn it off. Caulice!
	SYLVIE switches the radio off: Silence.
THERESE	*(as ETIENNE)* It's time for bed.
SYLVIE & JOSEE	But Pappa, it's only 9.30.
MARIETTE	I'm not tired.
THERESE	*(as ETIENNE)* You know the rules.
CHORUS	Yes, Pappa.
	They start to file past ETIENNE. He puts his hand up.
THERESE	*(as ETIENNE)* What about my goodnight kiss, eh?
	The girls file past ETIENNE, giving him goodnight kisses.
CHORUS	One *(SYLVIE)*, Two *(MARIETTE)*, Three *(JOSEE)*, Four *(ADELE)*
THERESE	Five.
CHORUS	Goodnight, Pappa.

THERESE   *(as ETIENNE)* Sweet dreams.

In unison they wipe his kisses off their cheeks. The other four walk past SYLVIE and sit in two rows of two.

1949. A schoolroom. SYLVIE transforms to schoolteacher.

SYLVIE   *(as TEACHER)* Some numbers have special properties. Like the number 9, for instance. It always multiplies and adds back up to itself. For example, 9 x 2 = 18; and, 1 + 8 = 9. And so forth.

MARIETTE   Does it always do that?

SYLVIE   *(as TEACHER)* Yes, it does. What's 9 x 7? Mariette?

MARIETTE   63.

SYLVIE   *(as TEACHER)* And...

MARIETTE   And, 6 + 3 = 9. Does it work for any other number?

SYLVIE   *(as TEACHER)* No, not in that way. Now girls, you try it. All the way up the 9 times table.

JOSEE, ADELE and THERESE begin to say the table as underscore. MARIETTE puts her hand up.

MARIETTE   Sister? Sister? I have a question.

SYLVIE   *(as TEACHER)* Yes, Mariette. What is it?

MARIETTE   What about the other numbers?

SYLVIE   *(as TEACHER)* What other numbers?

MARIETTE   I don't know...5. Does it have a special property?

SYLVIE   *(as TEACHER)* Why, yes it does. A peculiar one. When you add 5 to itself, it always ends with 5 or zero. Try it.

MARIETTE	5, 10, 15, 20, 25. Why does it do that?
SYLVIE	That's just its special property.
MARIETTE	Doesn't it ever change?
SYLVIE	*(as TEACHER)* No. It's always five or nothing. How are the rest of you doing?
CHORUS	Fine. *(they stop to listen)*
MARIETTE	But that's not fair. What if it just wants to be itself? Just one?
SYLVIE	*(as TEACHER)* It's still five.
MARIETTE	I don't like that rule.
SYLVIE	*(as TEACHER)* Well, that's just the way it is. It's not there for you to like or not. Numbers aren't human, Mariette. They don't have feelings. Now, could we change the subject please?
	Light change. The big house, 1950. ADELE and THERESE transform to MANON and ETIENNE. ETIENNE browses through a "Life" magazine. SYLVIE, JOSEE and MARIETTE sit looking away from their parents.
	Oppressive silence, broken by MARIETTE.
MARIETTE	Why do you hate us so much? We can't make any friends, we don't get to go out alone, we're not even allowed to go into town and buy shampoo.
SYLVIE	I think what Mariette is saying, Maman, is that we need a little more independence, even just around the house.
MARIETTE	These clothes are horrible! Nobody else in the family has to wear clothes like these.

JOSEE	Lisette gets to buy her own clothes, she gets to go into town and see her friends. She even gets to date.
MARIETTE	What if we want to go on dates? You never give a thought to what we might want.
THERESE	*(as ETIENNE)* Don't yell at your Mother!
ADELE	*(as MANON)* We're just trying to protect you.
SYLVIE	From what?
THERESE	*(as ETIENNE)* Out there. There are many hurtful people out there, just waiting to get you.
ADELE	*(as MANON)* You have to understand, girls. We love you so much.
THERESE	*(as ETIENNE)* You belong in the family. You're better off here.
MARIETTE	Then why did you give us away in the first place?
ADELE	*(as MANON)* They took you.
SYLVIE	You were happy to get rid of us. Isn't that the truth?
THERESE	*(as ETIENNE)* Where did you get an idea like that?
JOSEE	Oh, Pappa, that's all we ever hear.
SYLVIE	It's true, Maman, isn't it? You couldn't take care of us, so you let us go.
ADELE	*(as MANON)* You'll never understand. They took you. Even your father could not stop them.
THERESE	*(as ETIENNE)* There was nothing we could do. Those people were evil.
MARIETTE	No one else would let it happen.
JOSEE	If you wanted us, you would have kept us.

SYLVIE	How could you let your own children go? I want to understand, Maman, I really do.
ADELE	*(as MANON)* You'll never know what we went through because of you! What we did for your sake.
THERESE	*(as ETIENNE)* You're not like other children.
ADELE	*(as MANON)* You're cruel and heartless.
SYLVIE	That's not true.

> *In unison, the five reach in their pockets and find their coloured hair bows. They hold them to their hearts and then drop them like hot coals.*

> *Abruptly, mood changes to a bright but intimate atmosphere.*

JOSEE	Why the long face, Sylvie?
SYLVIE	I'm thinking.
MARIETTE	About what?
SYLVIE	About getting away from here — really away. I'm thinking of going to Montreal.
THERESE	What?
SYLVIE	I said, I want to go to Montreal.
THERESE	Why? *(beat)* Sylvie, why?
SYLVIE	Therese, we've finished school. It's time to go out and make our mark on the world.
MARIETTE	And what do you think you're going to do in the big city?
SYLVIE	Go to art college. I want to become a painter.
MARIETTE	You want to be an artist?

ADELE	Sylvie, that's wonderful.
JOSEE	Yes it is. But do you think Maman and Pappa will let you go?
SYLVIE	We're 18, Josee. It's time. How can they stop us?
MARIETTE	They can't. They'll try, but they can't. Not legally. *(theatrically)* We'll fight them in the courts, in the papers, on the beaches
CHORUS	*(á la WINSTON CHURCHILL)* We will never surrender!
SYLVIE	What about the rest of you?
THERESE	I thought that we would all stay here.
MARIETTE	And do what?
THERESE	I don't know. Maybe go into the Convent.
JOSEE	You mean, be nuns?
THERESE	I guess so. I can't imagine doing anything else.
SYLVIE	That's not true. We've all talked about our dreams.
JOSEE	That was sort of like make believe, Sylvie. I can't think of anything I'd be able to do.
THERESE	Neither can I.
MARIETTE	There's lots of things to do! What about you, Adele? You're so quiet.
ADELE	I'm going to enroll as a postulant at the Convent of the Sacred Virgin. I've already spoken to Mother Superior about it.
SYLVIE	Adele! You've been making plans behind our backs, you little sneak.

ADELE   That's not true, Sylvie. You know about my passion.

MARIETTE   Good for you, Adele. But I don't think I'm cut out for the religious life.

JOSEE   Me either.

SYLVIE   But you've got to do something! You can't just stay around here.

JOSEE   I guess I'll stay put. For a while, anyway. Until something comes to mind. Or someone.

MARIETTE   We'll finally get to go to town. On our own.

JOSEE   Maybe we'll fall in love!

THERESE   But you've never even dated before.

MARIETTE   So, we'll start now.

THERESE   Maman said that was not for us.

MARIETTE   What does she know? Why should we be different than anyone else? I'll do as I please.

JOSEE   And so will I.

THERESE   And me too.

SYLVIE   You'll have to come and visit me in the city. I might get lonesome.

ADELE   You're so brave, Sylvie. I'd be frightened in the city.

THERESE   Sylvie and Adele are going far away, on far away adventures.

ADELE begins to lose focus.

MARIETTE   I'm going too.

SYLVIE   What?

MARIETTE	I have to get away. It'll be hell around here without all of you.
THERESE	You'll all leave me, I know it.
SYLVIE	No, Therese. We're going to be free, think about that.
JOSEE	I'll stay, Therese. For a little while, anyway.
THERESE	It'll be strange not to see your faces around.
SYLVIE	Very strange. *(pause)* Are you alright, Adele?
ADELE	It's just one of my headaches.
JOSEE	Nothing will ever be the same again.
MARIETTE	Thank God for that! It's about time our ship came in.

ADELE collapses.

SYLVIE	Adele, what is it, what's wrong?
ADELE	I had a stomache ache. And then my bleeding started.
SYLVIE	That was a long time ago.
ADELE	But now my head hurts so much, I'm afraid it's going to burst. I want to take my vows. But I'm afraid.
SYLVIE	What are you talking about?
ADELE	What will I do without you? Who will staunch the blood?
SYLVIE	There's not going to be any blood, Adele.
ADELE	I won't be able to live without you.
SYLVIE	Yes, you will. You have so much faith, you're braver than the rest of us.
ADELE	It's a sign from God, Sylvie. That we shouldn't part.

SYLVIE	Don't worry. Saint Therese will take care of us.
THERESE	That's right, Adele.
JOSEE	You'll be fine.
MARIETTE	Adele, we'll visit you in the Convent.
SYLVIE	We'll always be there for each other. Always. Everything is going to be wonderful. From now on, everything will be wonderful. Believe me.
ADELE	I believe, Sylvie. Everything will be fine. If I could just close my eyes.

> *SYLVIE, MARIETTE, JOSEE and THERESE hold ADELE, who closes her eyes. Fade to black. End of Part One.*

Part Two

1955. SYLVIE, sophomore art student, is
dressed in a smock. She is attempting to
paint an abstract floral deconstruction. The
canvas is thick with paint. Behind her on a
small stool rests an open box of oils. Posed
in front of her are THERESE, MARIETTE,
JOSEE and ADELE in a group.

SYLVIE   How can you understand a flower?
To look at a plant that's full and ripe is
overwhelming;
The shape, colour, smell and texture of it.
The way the stalk and leaves are formed.
Each bit different, yet part of the whole.
But get inside that bloom and travel down
Down through
You'll come to the roots and seed of it all
And that seed sits tight inside the earth
Guarding what it wants to be
Dependent on combined qualities of soil, rain and
temperature
To help it open up.

And no matter what these qualities are like
Good or bad
For better or worse
It must germinate.
That's the rule of life.

*SYLVIE looks at her painting then goes
into her case and pulls out paper and
scissors. She cuts a string of paper dolls.
The other girls, led by ADELE, begin to
disperse leaving THERESE alone.
THERESE transforms to ETIENNE.*

ADELE *(singing)* J'entends le moulin, ticque ticque tacque
J'entends le moulin, tacque
J'entends le moulin, ticque ticque tacque
J'entends le moulin, tacque

Mon pere a fait batir maison
Ticque tacque, ticque tacque

J'entends le moulin, etc.

Sont trois charpentiers qui l'a fait
Ticque tacque, ticque tacque

J'entends le moulin, etc.

THERESE *(as ETIENNE)* Oh, they are golden to me, my
beautiful girls
As strong and golden as the fields in August.
But they have been taken away too soon
Too soon
My other children grow strong and tall
They ripen under the sun
But my five girls, no.
They are pale lilies cut down and left to rot
In someone else's house.

*THERESE transforms back to Quint.
SYLVIE has been cutting the dolls apart.
When the last two are separated, ADELE
begins speaking. Convent of the Sacred
Virgin.*

ADELE Please listen to me. You can let me go. I'm not really
sick, I just need to rest.

I can't settle down with these straps on. Please take
them off. They're making me crazy.

ADELE   I won't. I won't have another one if I can just get
               some rest. You don't even have to watch me, just
               stay with me.

               I've had seizures for a long time. I'll let you know if
               one comes on. I promise you I'll tell. Don't leave me
               alone!

               Why won't you listen?

               (praying) Saint Therese, the little flower
               Please pick me a rose from the heavenly garden
               Send it to me with a message of love
               That God may grant my wish
               O Saint Therese of the Baby, pray for us
               Saint Therese of the Baby, hear our prayer
               Saint Therese, little flower, priez pour nous

                         ADELE stops praying. She convulses and
                         chokes, lies still. A bell tolls faintly. The
                         four others look up.

MARIETTE   Adele.

JOSEE   Adele.

THERESE   Adele.

SYLVIE   Adele!

                         The bell stops tolling. ADELE transforms
                         to MANON, stands regarding four remaining
                         Quints with folded arms. She does not speak
                         with the chorus.

CHORUS   What are you talking about?

JOSEE   What are you telling us? Adele is dead?

CHORUS   How can that be?

SYLVIE   How can Adele be dead while I live?

THERESE	It's not true. No, no, it isn't true. I am alive and so is she. Unless I am dead. But if I'm dead, then where is she? The others are here.
MARIETTE	She is at the Convent.
JOSEE	She is at the Convent and she is going to take her vows. You're just trying to upset us again.
MARIETTE	This is just a bad joke.
SYLVIE	Smile and tell us that it's a joke.
THERESE	Please.
CHORUS	Oh, sweet Mary My twin and my mirror
SYLVIE	The glass is broken: the reflection is gone
CHORUS	I do not exist.
	ADELE, THERESE and MARIETTE retreat. SYLVIE takes her painting and hangs it on the wall, then shuts the dolls inside her paint box. JOSEE transforms to TEACHER and steps forward.
JOSEE	*(as TEACHER)* Come on in, Sylvie.
SYLVIE	Thank you. I'm sorry to disturb you.
JOSEE	*(as TEACHER)* That's alright. What can I do for you?
SYLVIE	Well, Mlle. Lalonge, it's that I've decided to leave school, and I want to go now.
JOSEE	*(as TEACHER)* But the term is nearly over, and you've only got another year to complete your certificate.
SYLVIE	I know, but I don't want to continue. It's making me crazy.

JOSEE	*(as TEACHER)* What is?
SYLVIE	Painting. There's too much insanity. I can't stand the way it makes me feel when I'm doing it. Then I look at what I've done, and I want to be sick.
JOSEE	*(as TEACHER)* But that's part of it, a part of the process. There is a certain chaos that cannot be avoided.
SYLVIE	Then I don't want it. I can't stand it. It's not for me. I need order.
CHORUS	What are you afraid of, Sylvie?
SYLVIE	I'm not afraid. *(pause)* I'm sorry, I don't mean to be rude. But you see, my mind is made up.
JOSEE	*(as TEACHER)* I see. What are your plans?
SYLVIE	I don't know. I want to find something with order, where I can apply myself.
JOSEE	*(as TEACHER)* Here you've been fighting hard, grasping for truth, fulfilling a dream, and you want to throw it away for order?
SYLVIE	I don't think I'm throwing anything away.
JOSEE	*(as TEACHER)* You'll become complacent.
SYLVIE	Don't tell me! You don't know how I feel.
JOSEE	*(as TEACHER)* You're absolutely right. I don't. Whatever it is that you do, you will keep painting? Sylvie?
SYLVIE	It doesn't matter.
JOSEE	*(as TEACHER)* Yes, it does. Look, Sylvie, I know you've had a tough time of it —
SYLVIE	I don't want to talk about this —

JOSEE	*(as TEACHER)* But you have talent.
SYLVIE	Thank you.
JOSEE	*(as TEACHER)* Your work shows a real relationship to the natural world and your technique is improving. It just seems such a waste —
SYLVIE	How would I ever be able to represent anything natural? *(pause)* Look, I'm sorry. It's nothing you can help me with.
JOSEE	*(as TEACHER)* I'm only trying to say that you could have a future as an artist. But it takes commitment.
SYLVIE	I know.
JOSEE	*(as TEACHER)* You have half credits for this term. You may pick up your courses whenever you wish. Do you understand what I'm saying? You are welcome back here any time.
SYLVIE	I appreciate this, Mlle. Lalonge. Thank you. Goodbye.
JOSEE	*(as TEACHER)* Farewell, Sylvie.

JOSEE watches SYLVIE leave, then exits.

Lights down on everyone but MARIETTE, whose dress affects beatnik-style. She beats on a small set of bongo drums.

MARIETTE	i feel the city heart beat - beat, baby its pulsing just for me

i shed no tears
as i bid goodbye
to your pallet of green (green algae slime-rot)
Ontario! flat canvas
here on the street
i make mi own scene
i feel the city heart beat
its pulsing just for me

MARIETTE
> i shed no tears
> as i bid goodbye
> to i - one of five (re-press womb no room to share)
> product of a fecund dream
> now i re-create miself
> i re-awake miself
> i see daylight in a din
> i feel the city heart beat
> its pulsing just for me
>
> and i, washed clean
>
> pathetic creature, dare you dream
> of another beat, a pulse in time
> a heart whose rhythm matches mine
>
> and do i have
> what it takes
> to feel mi own heart beat
> and match it to the street?

> *She stops drumming.*

MARIETTE   So, what do you think?

> *Lights down on MARIETTE, up on JOSEE.*

JOSEE   I'm at the salon, getting my hair done. It's my favourite thing to do. I love the way they dig their fingers in when they wash your hair! The style is a French Twist. After it's done and paid for, I can't resist going into the shop next door to try on a dress. An evening gown. Yellow silk. Strapless. A real knockout. *(striking a glamour pose)* Oh, I won't buy it. It's far too expensive, and where would I ever wear it? *(beat)* Now listen to this part. This guy — no, not a guy, a Man — stops to watch me. Does he know? Can he see Quintuplet? No. NO! He doesn't recognize me. I'm just a woman to him. One woman. Normal. Unique. *(holding out her hand)* Oh no, Robert, is it? I can't accompany you to tea. I already have a date. I'm so sorry. *(laughing luxuriously)* What an effort it is to tear myself out of that dress and get back into my pumpkin — I mean, my car.

> *Lights down on JOSEE, up on THERESE.*
> *A private hospital, early 1960's. ADELE*
> *transforms to a NURSE, approaching her*
> *with a syringe.*

ADELE   *(as NURSE)* Are we ready?

THERESE   Yes. *(beat)* What's that for?

ADELE   *(as NURSE)* It's sodium pentothal. It'll help you to relax before we start the therapy.

THERESE   You're sure it'll work. The therapy.

ADELE   *(as NURSE)* It will help you function normally.

THERESE   Will it make me happy?

ADELE   *(as NURSE)* Electroconvulsive therapy works in 95% of all these depression cases. You did request the treatment, Miss.

THERESE   I just wanted to make sure. Because my sister died during a convulsion.

> *ADELE as NURSE injects THERESE, who*
> *moves behind the bed. She and ADELE see*
> *one another through it. Lights down on*
> *them, and up on MARIETTE. MUSIC:*
> *from "Blue Rondo A La Turk" by Dave*
> *Brubeck.*

MARIETTE   So he says, "Say it." And I say, "Fuck." Oh, my God. Now I'll go to HELL for sure. And we lie there smoking a cigarette. And I start laughing, thinking, "My God, I did it." And I tell him that. "I can't believe I did it." And he says I've led a sheltered existence. He can tell because I'm so obsessively rebellious. That's cool. Then he starts talking about my sisters. My sisters. Now I'm starting to get razzed. "What are you talking about? How do you know my sisters?" He says, "Because that's all you ever talk about. It don't take no private dick to figure it out." So there it is. Written all over me. Paquette.

MARIETTE "So," he says, "Are they all as much fun as you?" What a thing to say! "Is that why you dated me? So you could have sex with a freak? Is that what you think? Isn't that what everyone thinks?" He just lays back and looks at me. "You're going to have to grow a thicker skin if you want to make it out there. Give me that smoke. It doesn't look as good on you as I do." Really. Goes by the name of Armand, dig!

> *Lights down on MARIETTE. ADELE sings one phrase of "Kyrie Eleison."*

> *SYLVIE enters, dressed in a nun's habit with Sacred Heart on the surplice. She carries a standing tray on which a small tea is set. A convent. JOSEE joins her. Lights on SYLVIE.*

CHORUS Shiny, shiny white and silver.
Streamlined surfaces.
Starched collars, freshly laundered nightgowns, and the scent of Lysol on a chilling breeze.

SYLVIE These are the clear, unsullied memories of my childhood and the life that I have regained. I am at home in the Convent. I understand the familiarity of order and the sane regime of schedule. This is sweet. The bell ringing for Lauds is the same cooling breeze that disinfects my existence every morning. I haven't fled the world — don't think that. It's just that my place in it is different. Happiness does not exist for we five — we four. I have a different path to tread. In this world where there is so much pain, and so little love, my path leads to a crystalline plateau between heaven and earth. That is all my faith and my desire.

> *SYLVIE sets the tea down and pulls the stool over. Lights now include JOSEE, seated. SYLVIE pours tea.*

JOSEE Sylvie, do you want to feel my belly?

SYLVIE What?

JOSEE	I said, do you want to feel my belly?
SYLVIE	No! *(beat)* That is, it's hardly the place. I mean, I would feel too strange...do you think it would be alright?
JOSEE	Of course. No one's here to see go ahead.

SYLVIE touches JOSEE's belly. She pulls back.

SYLVIE	Oh!
JOSEE	What is it?
SYLVIE	It's so hard. Not what I thought it would be.
JOSEE	What were you expecting?
SYLVIE	I don't know. Something softer, I guess.
JOSEE	Like Maman?
SYLVIE	No. Not like her.
JOSEE	Well, it certainly isn't soft.

SYLVIE touches her again.

SYLVIE	It's so round. So perfect.
JOSEE	Robert says I'm glowing like a Madonna.
SYLVIE	Does he.
JOSEE	But I just feel fat, like a pig. It's a little piglet. Oink!

They laugh.

SYLVIE	That's not a very nice thing to say about your baby.

Pause. SYLVIE sips tea.

JOSEE	Sylvie, the Doctor says I'm going to have twins.

SYLVIE   What?

JOSEE   Yes, twins. I don't know if I can care for one baby,
         let alone two. What if they're carbon copies of each
         other? I couldn't bear that. I just don't know if I'm
         capable of being a mother.

SYLVIE   You can always put them in a nursery.

JOSEE   Don't say that.

SYLVIE   I'm just kidding!

JOSEE   You probably think this shouldn't have happened.

SYLVIE   Did I say that?

JOSEE   You probably think we all should have taken vows.

SYLVIE   That's not true.

JOSEE   It's what Maman used to say, isn't it? That we
         mustn't take on this part of life? But it's what I want.
         Sylvie, it's what I need.

SYLVIE   I think you must seek what you need. And you have.
         You've found it.

JOSEE   That doesn't mean I'm not afraid. God! How am I
         supposed to raise these children? I don't know
         anything. All those things that mothers help their
         daughters with — I haven't been given anything. I
         have no experience. Can't you help me?

SYLVIE   How am I supposed to help you? I don't know
         anything either.

JOSEE   You used to. You always had words, good words.
         You made us believe in ourselves.

SYLVIE   Josee, I don't know. What am I supposed to say? That
         everything will be perfect? Yes. No. Maybe. Wait and
         see.

JOSEE	That's not much, coming from you.
SYLVIE	Whatever happens, I'm sure you'll deal with it.
JOSEE	I'm sure I will. *(beat)* At least I have something to deal with.
SYLVIE	And what is that supposed to mean?
JOSEE	Nothing.
SYLVIE	Excuse me, Josee. *(getting up)*
JOSEE	Sylvie, come back. I'm sorry. You're my sister! Sylvie!
SYLVIE	What!
JOSEE	Just give me your support. Let me know you'll be there. How difficult can that be?

> *SOUND: Buzz of cocktail crowd. Mid 1960's. THERESE appears, carrying flowers. MARIETTE and JOSEE join her. SYLVIE remains seated. ADELE remains standing.*

THERESE	If I could have everyone's attention — Hello? Hello! I want to welcome you all today to the opening of my store. It's such an honour to have everyone here today. Well, almost everyone. It's too bad Adele couldn't be here too to see the shop named after her. I love flowers. Did you know that when we were little girls, we each had our own flowers? That's right. Now, let me see if I can remember. Josee was Trillium. Mariette was a Daisy, and Sylvie was Forget-me-not, I think. Mine was more of a weed, the Queen Anne's lace, and Adele...Adele was Lily-of-the-valley.
MARIETTE	Therese, are you alright?

THERESE	Of course I am. I'm perfectly fine. I'm finally perfect. It's too bad I don't have any Lily-of-the-valley, but I do have carnations. White ones. And that's what everyone gets today for a remembrance.

> *THERESE pins a carnation on JOSEE, then MARIETTE. She still holds one in her hand.*

JOSEE	Therese, are you sure you're okay?
THERESE	You have to give remembrances when you open a store. Especially when it's named after your sister.
JOSEE	It's so morbid.
MARIETTE	Therese, have you been drinking?
THERESE	Silly. Don't you worry about me. I'm fine. I'm just a late bloomer.

> *ADELE transforms to REPORTER.*

ADELE	*(as REPORTER)* May I have a word with you, Miss Paquette?
THERESE	Yes! Yes, of course you may.
ADELE	*(as REPORTER)* Do you have any special hopes for your business?
THERESE	Yes, I do. *(handing ADELE the last carnation)* I hope that my flowers will brighten people's days, maybe even change their lives a little. And I want to keep the memory of my sister fresh.
ADELE	*(as REPORTER)* Why aren't your parents here at the opening?
THERESE	Well, I don't know how happy they were about my little business venture. But, it's my money to spend, right?
ADELE	*(as REPORTER)* And where does the money come from?

THERESE	The trust fund. You know, it's not a lot of money, but it's enough for my project.
ADELE	*(as REPORTER)* And how have you prepared yourself for the world of business?
THERESE	Well, I have this capital, and I'm eager to be a success. I certainly can't rely on the convent or school to shelter me. *(as ADELE begins to walk away)* I just have to make my own way, like everybody else.

> *JOSEE puts her hand on THERESE's shoulder.*

THERESE	Josee. Why didn't Sylvie come down today?
JOSEE	She's busy at the Convent, Therese. Preparing the novices for their vows. It's a bad time of the year.
THERESE	You're lying. She doesn't want to be with us any more.
JOSEE	That's not true.
MARIETTE	Don't be ridiculous, Therese.
THERESE	She's lucky. She made it by herself. The big sister.
MARIETTE	You can be such a baby!
JOSEE	Therese, I'm telling you. It's just the time of year. Easter is the hardest time.
THERESE	But it's a good time for flowers. You wait, Josee, Mariette — I'll be a big success by the end of the year. Madame Therese Paquette — a famous florist.

> *Lights down. THERESE exits. A dim light remains on her. Lights on JOSEE. She speaks to SYLVIE and MARIETTE.*

JOSEE   I wanted — I want — to turn fear into hope, and if
         that means challenging God, then so be it. To create
         life, to go on — it's not such a big dream, is it? I
         was so afraid to open up and give birth — afraid that I
         wouldn't be able to take the pain, that I'd split in two,
         that some terrible thing would come roaring out of
         me. Monsters breed monsters, don't they? And I'd be
         punished somehow for daring to go against
         everything I was taught. But that's not what
         happened. I gave birth to two beautiful baby boys,
         carbon copy cherubs. Five fingers, five toes, two
         individuals. Perfect in every way. Except for one
         small thing. A kidney problem with one of my sons.
         (beat) I will not have my child grow up in a hospital.
         Michel will be taken off the dialysis. Oh, my poor
         baby boy.

                    SYLVIE stands aside.

SYLVIE   Mother Superior says that life is a series of trials to
         which we are subjected, and I know this to be true.
         God makes hardships for us, and Mary makes them
         easier to bear. Faith doesn't require proof, but I have
         it. Sometimes I wake up in the night, my heart
         pounding, just terrified...the Sandman...but then I
         pray to Mary, who is good, and pure, and she gets me
         through my bad feelings so that I can sleep again. I
         know that there are people who don't believe. I pity
         them. My life is much better than it might be
         because Mary, the divine Mother, keeps the Sandman
         away. I have faith. *(less certain)* I do believe.

                    Lights stay up on SYLVIE and come up on
                    THERESE. The flower shop. She holds a
                    huge bouquet of flowers.

THERESE Outside it's January, dead winter. But inside here, it's
         always springtime. Just the flowers and me. That's
         the best thing about a regulated environment. You
         never have to worry about change.

                    Lights down on THERESE. She exits.
                    Lights up on MARIETTE.

MARIETTE   Sisters, sisters, sisters, sisters and sisters again! How
              am I supposed to explain it to him? I married a
              perfect saxophone boy whose tongue spoke the
              language of pure jazz. This boy whose tongue taught
              me to love and to be loved. This boy whose tongue
              licked me back to life when I was a poor, ignorant,
              scalded whelp. This man who loves me
              unconditionally, despite my sisters. My all invasive,
              all-pervasive sisters. We had seven years of pure jazz
              love but now I find that a life of two is incomplete.
              After struggling so hard against the grain I need that
              manifold reflection of myself. That community.
              "Sisters," he says, "it's them or me. And I don't think
              it's me you need. But Mariette, it's up to you.

                        *SYLVIE, MARIETTE, JOSEE and ADELE
                        are now each dimly lit. Lights up on
                        THERESE's shop, which is empty of
                        flowers. THERESE enters, carrying a glass.*

THERESE   Gone. It's all gone. My sisters, my home and my
              health. My flower shop. Everything that ever meant
              something to me. Gone. Vanished. Poof! By the will
              of God. "God wills it, and it must be so." But you are
              not a just God. I believe in you God, I do, but you
              are not just. What you have done is not just. Why did
              the sisters say that everyone must suffer? It's not true.
              Everyone does not suffer, not the way I have. We
              were nothing to you. Why for the love of Jesus did
              you put us here? To show people how ugly nature is?
              To make everyone else happy that they were not us?
              Or were you just a little short on ideas for jokes? I
              know what that's like. I'm a little short too. On
              money, love, and patience.

SYLVIE   Patience.

THERESE   A little low on hope.

SYLVIE   Hope.

THERESE   But what I do have is a drink and *(reaching into her pocket and pulling out a pill bottle)* some pretty little rosary beads. A promise of redemption — just enough to restore my will. Not your will, God. Mine. And I will that one thing, just one thing I do, is going to be good, and right, and just. *(popping the lid off the bottle)* And fail safe. You see, God, I don't have time for your second big decision.

　　　　　　　She pours the pills into her hand.

　　　　　　　Here's to me, God. I am Therese Helene Paquette, fifth of five. *(spilling the pills)* I will it, and it must be so.

　　　　　　　A telephone rings and rings until MARIETTE appears in the shop, followed by SYLVIE and JOSEE. SYLVIE no longer wears her habit. MARIETTE sees THERESE lying on the floor.

MARIETTE   Oh Jesus.

SYLVIE   Oh my dear God.

JOSEE   What's the matter? What's wrong with her?

MARIETTE   Josee, don't look.

SYLVIE   Mariette. Don't. She's gone.

MARIETTE   Peewee.

JOSEE   Oh Jesus. Oh God.

SYLVIE   Mariette, don't touch her. We have to call an ambulance. The police.

MARIETTE   *(kneeling beside THERESE)* Not the police! Oh, little sister.

SYLVIE   Josee, call an ambulance.

MARIETTE   That's me lying there.

SYLVIE   Less and less.

>   *THERESE rises and looks at her sisters.*
>   *ADELE appears and beckons. THERESE*
>   *goes to her.*

THERESE   Blessed Saint Therese, little flower
                All my life I've been waiting for your promise to be
                fulfilled.
                Lead me now to my sister, my twin.
                My angel.
                Now the glass is restored.
                I'm home.

>   *Lights fade on ADELE and THERESE.*
>   *MARIETTE, JOSEE and SYLVIE standing*
>   *at THERESE's gravesite.*

MARIETTE   Josee, stop fidgeting.

JOSEE   There is mud all over my shoes. I just bought
                these shoes, and now they're filthy.

MARIETTE   Shut up you. Who cares about your shoes.

JOSEE   Not you, that's certain.

SYLVIE   What a stupid thing to say.

JOSEE   I don't care about my shoes.

MARIETTE   I know.

SYLVIE   It shouldn't have been her.

MARIETTE   What?

SYLVIE   Anyone else. Not her.

JOSEE   Sylvie, come on.

SYLVIE   Where is everyone today? Where are they? Where's
                our big happy family?

MARIETTE	Stop it.
SYLVIE	Where's our loving mother? She wept big tears for Adele.
JOSEE	Sylvie, you know she's not well.
SYLVIE	If she cared she would have come. It should have been her.
MARIETTE	Stop it right now. Come on, Sylvie. We've got each other. All we need right here.
JOSEE	Just like it's always been.
SYLVIE	No. Don't hang on me. Leave me alone. I'm sick of you...I don't want to be a part of it any more. Just leave me alone.
JOSEE	What do you mean?
SYLVIE	Adele and Therese are much better off, don't you think?
MARIETTE	Now you're being ridiculous.
SYLVIE	They're free.
JOSEE	I don't want to listen to this.
SYLVIE	Our lives are meaningless. They mean nothing. We're nothing.
JOSEE	You're wrong.
SYLVIE	It's the truth. Hard candy.
JOSEE	You bitch.
MARIETTE	What is your problem, Sylvie? What is the matter with you? Tell us. *(pause)* Nothing, you say. Nothing. You've got nothing to say, and that right there is your problem. Isn't that right?

JOSEE	How dare you say those things to us? We've loved you, shared with you, cared for you —
MARIETTE	Oh yes, you've really tried, haven't you. In school, out of school. You're in the convent, you're out of the convent. You can't commit to anything. To being someone. Why? I'll tell you. You never grew up, you never made it past the fence of that goddamned observation ground. Don't you dare rail at your sister there who has tried, who has lived, who has known love and borne children. Who has seen her child die! That is something. What have you got?
SYLVIE	I have a life. I have dreams.

> *JOSEE and MARIETTE speak simultaneously.*

MARIETTE	What is your life? Tell me.
JOSEE	Who are you, Sylvie?
SYLVIE	You never listen to me. I don't know. *(beat)* Please tell me, if you can, if you have ever taken five seconds to think about life in all your running around trying to live it. You're right. I'm having a little problem here, sisters. The merry-go-round stopped and I forgot to get off. Why should I? It was such a perfect ride while it lasted, my big blue cat with a violet painted on its side. I can't get off, because I'll fall and I'm afraid that no one will be there to catch me.
	Who will help me if I'm hurt. If I bleed, who will take care of me?
JOSEE	It's the same for us, Sylvie. It's just that we've gone on.
SYLVIE	With what? With what? *(pause)* There is less and less to go on all the time.

> *JOSEE and MARIETTE do not answer.*
> *SYLVIE leaves them at the grave. Lights*
> *down on them, up on SYVLIE pacing back*
> *and forth. The flower painting and her paint*
> *case are nearby.*

SYLVIE   Left behind. I've been left behind. I've spent so much time trying to put everyone behind me that I've lost myself. Mariette is right. Something's missing in me. I have to know who I am.

> *SYLVIE looks at her painting, then opens*
> *the case. She pulls out the five paper dolls.*

SYLVIE   Sylvie, Mariette, Josee, Adele, Therese. Away you go. *(throwing the dolls in the air — they flutter around her)* Before there were five, there was one. That's what Maman said. I just have to get back there.

> *SYLVIE finds her sketchbook and tears a*
> *sheet out of it, then scrambles around in the*
> *case and finds scissors. She folds the sheet*
> *into five and prepares to cut.*

SYLVIE   If I can only remember how to do this.

> *SYLVIE cuts into the paper. Her gestures*
> *are strong, determined. Lights fade on her*
> *and come up on THERESE.*

THERESE   *(as ETIENNE)* People all over the world stare at our girls and wonder what it means. The doctors say that my daughters are some kind of strange thing, a mistake that happened in my wife's womb. The priests tell us that the girls are a sign of God's will. The newspapers talk about providence. The government looks at them and sees money. But everyone wants to know, "How did this happen?" I don't know how. It just did. And it turned us inside out. Maybe in all that fuss we forgot how to love our girls. But at least there's this. They have got each other in a way that nobody else ever will. When there's not enough love from outside, I know that they will always have each other.

> *Lights fade on THERESE. MARIETTE and JOSEE at the cabin, as in Part One. SYLVIE meets them.*

SYLVIE   Josee, Mariette. I came as soon as I could.

MARIETTE   Go on, then. For yourself.

JOSEE   Go, Sylvie. For all of us.

> *SYLVIE goes to see MANON., but the bed is empty. SYLVIE pulls the covers up to the pillow and crosses herself.*

SYLVIE   Maman? Are you there? I didn't want to come back and see you. I wanted to put everything away from me, as far as possible. Everything. But now it's all going. Adele, Therese, Pappa, you. Maman? Please speak to me. Please be real for me, please come through just once. You offered a gift. It's time.

> *SYLVIE pulls the chain of dolls from her pocket. Light on ADELE, holding hands with THERESE. As SYLVIE listens to MANON she slowly unfolds the chain. MARIETTE and JOSEE enter and watch.*

ADELE   *(as MANON)* I am not an educated person. I don't know what all the doctors and scientists mean when they talk about odds and genetics and such things. But my girls, you ask why you are different so I will tell you what I believe. As I remember, when your father and I made you, the heat of our love melted that cold November. And I think that maybe there was just too much love to fit inside one little body. So when you came along the next spring, you came like the flowers. Not just one, but many little buds who just grew and grew and grew.

> *SYLVIE folds the dolls back into one. She places them on the bed.*

SYLVIE   Here's your little girl, Maman.

> *SYLVIE pats the bedcovers then finds a brown paper bag. She looks inside and begins to laugh.*

I don't believe it.

JOSEE What is it, Sylvie?

> *SYLVIE empties the bag into her hand. Some candy falls into her palm.*

SYLVIE We'll share.

> *As she gives candies to MARIETTE and JOSEE, lights fade to sunset and slowly to their individual colours. SYLVIE, MARIETTE and JOSEE are joined by ADELE and THERESE.*

JOSEE Mariette and Adele are so lucky. Look. Their colours are in the beautiful sunset.

MARIETTE But Josee, your colour is in the sunshine.

ADELE And Sylvie's is the big blue sky.

THERESE Where's mine? I can't see it at all.

MARIETTE It's underneath the snow, Therese.

SYLVIE Yes, Therese. When the snow melts, your colour will be all over the land.

JOSEE You'll be luckiest of all.

THERESE But when will the snow melt? Please tell me, Sylvie. You know about everything.

SYLVIE Now. Now everything is alive.

> *They move to their separate colour spaces.*

THERESE My name is Therese.

JOSEE   My name is Josee.

MARIETTE   My name is Mariette.

ADELE   My name is Adele.

SYLVIE   I am Sylvie.

> *All five sisters pop the candy into their mouths and chew it as lights fade.*
>
> *The End.*

No More Medea

In 1990, a young woman came to see this play at Factory Theatre and introduced herself as "Medea." As she spoke, my initial surprise and disbelief were replaced by feelings of sadness, hope, but most of all, wonder as this Greek expatriate told me her story.

Dedicated to the Medea of Toronto.

Production History

No More Medea was fisrt produced at Buddies in Bad Times Rhubarb
Festival, 1990 with the following cast:

MEDEA/DROWNED WOMAN	*Victoria Shaffelburg*
THE VIRGIN MARY/JASON	*Siobhan McCormick*

Directed by Deborah Porter.
Video by Deborah Porter and Susan Ross.
Stage managed by Veronica MacDonald.

No More Medea was expanded and produced by Particle-Zoo Productions
at the Fringe of Toronto Festival, June 1990, with the following cast:

MEDEA	*Ellen-Ray Hennessy*
THE VIRGIN MARY	*Siobhan McCormick*
DROWNED WOMAN	*Victoria Shaffleburg*

Directed and designed by Deborah Porter.
Stage managed by Rob Lewis.

No More Medea was first produced by Particle-Zoo Productions at
Factory Theatre Studio Cafe, November, 1990 with the following cast:

MEDEA	*Ellen-Ray Hennessy*
THE VIRGIN MARY	*Siobhan McCormick*
DROWNED WOMAN	*Victoria Shaffelburg*

Directed by Deborah Porter.
Stage Manager - Jennifer O'Connor
Set Designer - Deborah Porter
Costume Designer - Siobhan McCormick
Lighting Designer - Michel Charbonneau
Sound - Michel Charbonneau and Deborah Porter
Video - Deborah Porter and Susan Ross

The Settings

Corinth, Greece 3000 BC

A wasteland beyond time and space

Toronto, Canada 1990 AD (The third setting can replicate any major city in a current year.)

The Characters

MEDEA	a woman from Colchis
THE VIRGIN MARY *doubles as*	mother of Christ
PAN/DORA *and*	a statue
JASON	Medea's hapless husband

Notes

This play requires a broad acting style — have fun with portrayals.

If a woman named Medea did indeed live, love and murder her children 5,000 years ago, then surely she is still alive and still trying to survive in a society whose rules are not of her making. History repeats itself and ghosts walk the earth while their sorrows are embodied in the lives of the great and the small.

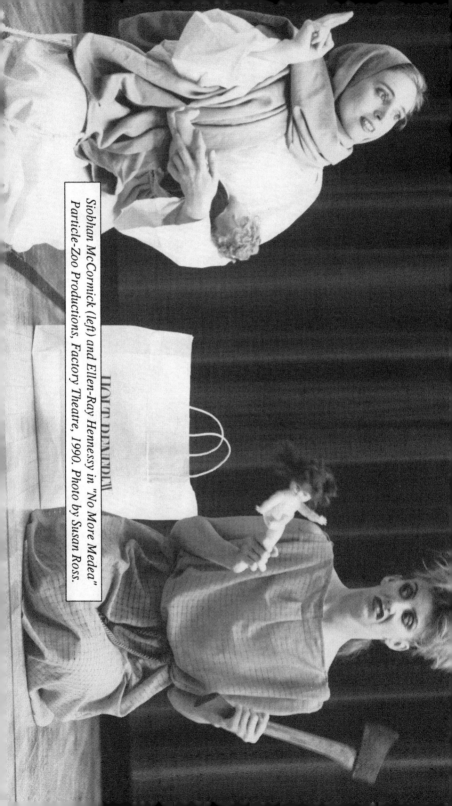

Siobhan McCormick (left) and Ellen-Ray Hennessy in "No More Medea" Particle-Zoo Productions, Factory Theatre, 1990. Photo by Susan Ross.

No More Medea

*Dark. Strong, tumultuous music. Lightning
flash and thunder. A statue is revealed on stage,
resplendent in toga and grapes. Blackout.
Lightning. Thunder. In the flash, the statue
starts to quiver. Blackout. Lightning. Thunder.
The statue is now shaking. Lights continue to
rise as the music crescendos. The statue comes
to life with a yell, dishevelled, minus a few
grapes.*

PAN/DORA Lay by! Forswear your songs of mortal woe
And tell no tales of man's dark dolorous grief
We must have action, spice and vitriol
Deep thoughts to think, and comical relief.
So settle back, suspend your disbelief:
And enter the ancient Hellenic realm — let's call it Greece
A full generation before Ulysses' odyssey.
A wondrous ram lies sacrificed,
Its fleece of gold pegged to a tree
And guarded by a serpent most malignant.
Jason is on a quest to seize it from a hostile king
Who'd rather see him dead than take the treasure —
All seems lost.
But Hera, Queen of Heaven, has taken pity on Jason
She bribes Cupid to let fly with his shaft of love
Straight into the heart of Medea, the King's daughter,
Herself a woman of great power *(thunder)*
Against her will she falls in love: with arts sublime
Helps Jason gain the Golden Fleece,
Then speeds his way back to the ship.
Her father follows close on their heels

And in her frenzy to help the Greek
She tears her brother limb from limb
Casting the shredded corpse behind.
The army slows to gather up the pieces;
And thus, the Argo flees cruel Colchis' shore.
Perhaps from pity, perhaps from fond amour,
Or gratitude for her assistance,
Jason takes her on board the ship, which is now bound for
Corinth.
She loves him with a passion most unseemly,
And he vows marriage and a happy home.
In time, two sons are born, product of their great affection
And all is well — till Jason, tiring of his 'foreign' mate
Forsakes her to marry the daughter of the Corinthian king.
Alone, cast off, this woman of great powers (Some say
Black Magic) *(thunder)* Ponders her imminent exile.

Thunder. PAN/DORA exits. MEDEA enters.

MEDEA   Aaaaagggghhhhh!!!!
If only Zeus would strike me dead this very instant *(thunder)*
Or better yet, strike *him* dead
That creep, that piggish liar, who with one move
Has betrayed me, betrayed our sons, made foul
All that is fair. And two more thunderbolts *(thunder)*
Would render ash the dissembler who calls himself a "king"
And his stinking daughter.
How dare that ingenue set herself against me, Medea,
Once princess myself, now noble wife and mother?
Was noble wife. Still mother
Could that which we call life be any worse?

*JASON enters, unseen by MEDEA. He wears
the Golden Fleece.*

MEDEA   A wife betrayed, a marriage bed annulled,
And me, alone with two small sons,
Sentenced to wander the wastes of a foreign land
This "Greece" — a greasy place.
My homeland shut to me — what shall I do?

JASON   A gracious start might be to shut your trap.

MEDEA   You! You stinking coward, dare return —

JASON   Shut up, Medea, and count your blessings where you can.
               Your situation here could have been nice enough
               Divorce, shared custody, a small allowance
               But news of your foul temper goes before you
               And that is why the King decreed this exile.

MEDEA   Let Creon answer to his actions.
               I want to know just where you get the gall
               To commit such foul adultery.
               I forsook my father, my homeland, all that I knew
               To give you aid — why, you owe everything to me!

JASON   Oh, now we're onto that again.
               Let's have a look at those brave deeds of yours you so
               revere.

MEDEA   Yes, let's.

JASON   I will admit, you showed some smarts, good common sense
               In helping me to overcome those...problems.

MEDEA   Problems?! Those were insurmountable obstacles
               The solutions to which lay far beyond your wit and scope!

JASON   Oh yeah? Like what?

MEDEA   Like — my magic stone that quelled the phantom army.

JASON   Yeah...

MEDEA   Like — my elixir that made you impervious to the sword.

JASON   Uh huh...

MEDEA   Like — the guardian snake I lulled to sleep with potent
               charm.

JASON   Okay, okay! You helped a little.

MEDEA   A lot.

JASON   A...lot.

MEDEA   You couldn't have done it without me. Admit it!

JASON   Alright. Your magic saved the day
And was the thing that got my Golden Fleece.
My lovely, lovely Fleece.
But then again, you were so overcome with passion
You acted without thinking. And passion doesn't count.

MEDEA   Passion doesn't count?

JASON   All men know that reason rules best.
Besides, I rescued you from that barbaric land
Which only now you fondly call your home.

MEDEA   Jason, your memory is just as faulty
As that other tool you wield to small effect.

JASON   To some effect, it seems, since we have made two boys
Who also stand to suffer from your overheated mouth
It brings to mind that nether heated mouth
Which guides your actions.

MEDEA   Oh, dull of wit, why were you sent to me?
Could Eros not have tipped his dart in braver seed?

JASON   Oh, it's a cruel trick of nature
That man alone cannot bestow the gift of life!
We'd save some trouble then, eh?

MEDEA   Save this, would you.

JASON   Ah well. Profound thoughts later. First, I'll see to you
I have made a case for you with Creon
To mitigate that cruel punishment
You'll find there's gold, and letters to speed you on the road
So exile's not such hardship after all.

MEDEA   My honour is not for sale.
Keep your coin and worthless signatures!
You still ignore that question which I first put to you
How could you overthrow the order of your house,
Defile all that was between us,
To wed this green and untried maid?

JASON   Look to yourself for the answer to that one, Lady.
As you know, both you and I are foreigners here
At least, I am a Greek; but you are from uncharted shores.
Our sons don't stand a chance of education, placement,
And all that makes young men seem fair.
I wed the princess to secure all that, and more
A surety for you in your sunset years.

MEDEA   Don't do me any favours. Jason, you pig!
I won't stand idly while you indulge yourself
And make a fool of me!

JASON   You don't need me for that.

MEDEA   Takes one to know one...

JASON   Harpy.

MEDEA   Gold-digger.

JASON   Witch! Virago!

MEDEA   You yellow-bellied, lily-livered, crown-sucking coward!

JASON   This fit of hysteria does not auger well
Nor does it become your fading charms.
I'll take my leave, and not return
Till word arrives that you have seen to reason.

MEDEA   Go on, Jason, on to your virgin fluff
And try to get it up, if you still can.

JASON   Medea, heed the time. Don't entertain ideas of revenge.
Your thoughts are wisely spent on your own safety.
Creon's justice is cruel, and swift
And you, my sweet are alone in hostile land.

JASON exits.

MEDEA   So.
Now we see what strong, true men are made of.
When going to the market, it's easy to tell
The good fruit from the soft and overripe:
But men are different things,
And many a fine exterior hides a weak and shameless heart.
Still, I suppose the fault is mine, for succumbing to
The bittersweet pain that is called love.
Never mind that now. What's done is done.
Besides, I'm "entertaining" the loveliest idea for revenge.
I'll call Jason back, and speak so soft
That he cannot refuse my small request. It goes like this:
"I've had a change of heart. Good luck, and I go willingly,
But let the children stay. They are too young to live
In that arid plain where I must be content."
I hate to use the kids as chattel in this battle;
But, I need them to fulfill my plan.
He will agree.
I'll send them to the palace with gifts for the bride:
A dress of silk, and coronet of gold,
Which I'll prepare and fill with the deadliest poison known
to man.
She'll gasp with pleasure, put them on —
And burn to death with most exquisite pain.
Any that touch her will also die, so potent is this venom!

And thus is made my vengeance on her and that oafish king.
Jason will be upset too, I know,
But I have further plans to deal with that traitor.
And surely now my mother's heart must shrivel up and die.
I'll kill the children.
Oh, Medea, what is wrong with you
That such a plan was ever born?
Your gentle babes! Their silken hair and rosy cheeks — stop!
But I see no other way.
They go with me — they die.
They stay — they'll die for sure.
My murder of the boys will save them from crueler hands,
And is the surest way to torture Jason.
Oh gods!
I won't be scorned or mocked as a spurned thing
I am of royal blood myself, grand-daughter of Apollo.
Many women take this kind of treatment as their due
And are forced to, in a world that hates our sex.

MEDEA   I am a different creature, and will not!
Oh yes — I'm foul, I am the vilest of women,
The nursing bitch who thwarts the trust of her pup.
Now, History: Come. Plot my course.
I'll be the monster for your books and plays
So be it. Seal my fate.

> *Blackout, and thunder. A great wind blows.*
> *Lights come up to reveal MEDEA in a*
> *"wasteland." She picks herself up and dusts*
> *herself off, looking around.*

MEDEA   Hello. Hello? Hello! Is anybody here? Where am I?

VOICE   The Place of Battered Legends...

MEDEA   What?

VOICE   The Place of Battered Legends...

MEDEA   You've got to be kidding.

VOICE   No...

> *MEDEA blows some dust off a piece of*
> *classical junk.*

MEDEA   Doomed. Doomed! Out of space and time.

> *MEDEA sits down, grows bored, and starts to*
> *snooze, but never really gets to sleep. Her*
> *posture and dreams are too uncomfortable.*
> *Time passes...a light wind blows.*

MEDEA   *(mumbling)* Jason, move over. You're hogging the
bed...Creon, you big fat pig, you'll get yours...Oh honey,
aren't the kids cute?...

> *We hear the sporadic cries of a woman in*
> *labour. MEDEA tries to ignore them until*
> *they become too loud and frequent.*

MEDEA   Shut up! SHUT UP!

> *The cries crescendo, then we hear a slap and a baby's wail. Silence. Satisfied, MEDEA settles down to sleep. Then the sound of creaking wood is heard. A bent cross rises, spinning round and round against the back wall.*

MEDEA What in Hades...

> *We hear a woman weeping and the cross disappears. A huge wind blows. MEDEA is tossed around by the force of it. THE VIRGIN MARY is blown on stage. MEDEA hides.*

MARY Gabriel...Michael...I'm here! Raphael...Yoo-hoo!

MEDEA Who, in Hades' foul name, are you?

MARY Why, I'm Mary.

MEDEA Who?

MARY Ma-ry. The Mother of Christ.

> *MEDEA sneaks up behind MARY.*

MEDEA Who?

MARY The Paschal Lamb.

MEDEA Doesn't ring a bell. Ding ding ding!

> *They see each other and scream.*

Hey! This fleecy lamb. It's not gold, is it?

MARY Why, no.

MEDEA Lucky for you.

MARY Are you a heathen?

MEDEA No.

MARY A Philistine?

MEDEA   Uh-uh.

MARY   Well, who are you then?

MEDEA   A Colcherian. From Colchis. A place near Greece.

MARY   Ah. A traveller.

MEDEA   Only in time. Hello Mary, the name's Medea. *(pronouncing it Med-ee-a)* Don't wear it out.

MARY   Why, hello, Medea. *(pronouncing it Med-ay-a)*

MEDEA   That's Medea! *(pause)* Mary, do you happen to know what year it is?

MARY   Since the death, about 10 years.

MEDEA   Whose death?

MARY   My son's.

MEDEA   Oh, really? And when did he die?

MARY   I just said, about 10 years ago.

MEDEA   Sorry. I'm just trying to get a handle on how long I've been here.

MARY   Where is here, exactly?

MEDEA   Didn't they tell you?

MARY   Nobody's told me a thing. Just a minute ago, I was giving succour to some poor unfortunate in Palestine when suddenly, whoosh! A gust of wind like to the breath of God blew me around and here I am! Where am I?

MEDEA   Welcome to the Place of Battered Legends! Where an exclusive collection of saints and sinners while away the eons as the dust grows heavy on our shoulders. So. What did you do?

MARY   Do?

MEDEA   To deserve this.

MARY   Deserve? I don't follow you.

MEDEA   Sit down. Look, Mary, I hate to be the one to break it to
              you, but you're dead. D-E-A-D. Literally.

MARY   I feel fine, though.

MEDEA   Well, figuratively, you're still alive, because I've been graced
              with your presence. So. What's the big secret? Your
              unspeakable crime?

MARY   I have no secrets.

MEDEA   Look. You're going to be spending a lot of time here, so
              you may as well come clean right now. Fess up. Spill the
              beans. What's your claim to infamy?

MARY   I only did what was required, no more, no less. I took my
              due, answered my calling...*(rapt, lost in reverie, she gazes
              heavenward)*

MEDEA   Yep, that'd be it. Mary. Mary. MARY!

MARY   The annunciation, the journey, the stable all forlorn; the
              birth, the betrayal, the assassination!

MEDEA   Yes! Good! That sounds exciting!

MARY   Oh no, it's not all mine. Just the mother part really. The
              Virgin Mother.

MEDEA   Yes well, you can tell me all about it sometime. There's
              plenty of that around here. Time. Time to go over and over
              it all. Lots of good stories, if you get in with the right
              crowd.

MARY   What do you mean, time to go over and over it?

MEDEA   Whatever you did to get here. They'll keep dredging your
        name up whenever possible. The people on earth. You'd
        think they'd have more to do than bother with us crusty old
        fossils. But no. They use your name and your story to suit
        their own ends. Myths, archetypes, a little light
        entertainment...Hah! Without any thought to what it puts us
        through! Ask Medusa, Helen, Jezebel —

MARY   *She's* here?

MEDEA   Hey! It's a wild bunch. You must have done something bad,
        Mary. Think. Everyone who's anyone in the annals of
        passion, crime and vengeance is present. And a few by
        default. Oh, you can't put a foot wrong. One teensy, tiny
        mistake, and — whoosh! The story just grows and grows.
        No merciful sleep for you! Such is the life of a legend.

MARY   Sounds like a bad lot. How can you all stand each other?

MEDEA   You see the strangest friendships forming. Then there's me.
        I've been alone for countless eons. They couldn't find my
        match. Now you've come. I don't understand. I thought I'd
        get some sort of monster; maybe a Hydra or all the Harpies.

MARY   Why? What did you do?

MEDEA   With a lunge and a lunge and a lunge lunge lunge I killed
        my sons. Oh, there were lots of other, wonderful things
        mixed in there too, but that's what it all centres on now. At
        least, that's what *they* all talk about.

MARY   You mean, with a lunge and a lunge and a lunge lunge lunge
        you killed your sons? *(as MEDEA shrugs)* Oh, my God.

MEDEA   Gets a great reaction every time.

MARY   But that's horrible! How could you?

MEDEA   It's a long story. It all started back in Colchis...*(but MARY
        shrinks away from her)* Get over it.

MARY   I think I've come to the wrong place. There must be some
        mistake. Help! *(beginning to pray)*

MEDEA   Mary? Mary? *(pause)* Looks like it's going to be an exciting millenium — or two.

> *Blackout. A strong wind blows. Lights up reveal MEDEA and MARY observing new characters entering their strange world, as suggested by some appropriately bizarre sound effects.*

MEDEA   Guinevere. Awww, look Mary. So sweet, so devout. Probably a better companion for you than me.

MARY   Jeanne d'Arc! Ahhh!

MEDEA   Lucretia Borgia?

MARY   That's disgusting.

MEDEA   Eva Braun! Crikey, they're dropping like flies today.

MARY   Must be the times.

MEDEA   Must be.

> *Pause.*

MARY   I think I'll go for a little stroll.

MEDEA   Oh? Where?

MARY   Earth.

MEDEA   And just how are you going to do that, Mary?

MARY   We can go back, you know.

MEDEA   We're stuck here.

MARY   We may be stuck with each other, *Medea*...

MEDEA   That's Medea!

MARY   ...but we don't have to stay put. Just the other century, while you were sulking, I took a little exploratory trip.

MEDEA   Really. I had no idea.

MARY   If you took more notice of your surroundings, you might discover something of interest. Anyway, I'm off.

MEDEA   To do what?

MARY   Take a look around, observe the penitents. See how things are going. *(pause)* Do you want to come?

MEDEA   Not on your life.

MARY   Suit yourself.

> *MEDEA watches MARY take off into the wind. Blackout. Wind blows. Lights up to reveal MEDEA dozing. MARY stands beside her with a small suitcase.*

MARY   I'm back.

MEDEA   So. *(pause)* How was it?

MARY   It was very curious. Greatly changed. And yet — not so different.

MEDEA   I'll just bet.

MARY   No really, you should see for yourself.

MEDEA   Not in a million years. *(seeing the suitcase)* What's that for?

MARY   I've packed a few small items. I'm going back for a bit and you're coming too. There's some things I think you should see. Get your mind off all this. Aren't you bored? *Medea...*

MEDEA   It's Medea!

MARY   I'm not going to allow you to sit here and stew until Doomsday!

MEDEA   Lay off.

MARY   Come on! It's fun! It's really fun. It's busy. There's loads of action, good and bad, lots of people, happy and sad, and...shopping.

MEDEA   What's that?

MARY   Trading goods, like in the old days, except it's much more interesting. More variety. People seem to really enjoy it. Let's give it a try.

MEDEA   It sounds dreadful.

MARY   That's it! I've had it with your lousy attitude. If I have to spend the rest of eternity with you, we're going to have a good time!

MEDEA   No, Mary. I don't want to go. Unknit thy brow, Mary.

MARY   Come on!

MEDEA   I don't think I should, Mary. Let go of me! Joy to the world...

MARY   Come on, *Medea!*

MEDEA   It's Medea!

MARY   COME ON!

> *Wind blows. Lights dim. MARY and MEDEA "take off" into the wind. Blackout. Lights come up to reveal them 'flying', facing the audience. MARY holds the suitcase, and she is a graceful flyer. MEDEA has rather more trouble.*

MARY   Isn't this fun?

MEDEA   A regular riot. Where are we going?

MARY   I'm not sure. We'll just have to wait and see where we land.

MEDEA   I refuse to set foot anywhere remotely near Greece.

MARY   Don't worry. It looks like we're heading for North America.

MEDEA   Where's that?

MARY   Over there, to the west. See that yellow film in the air?

MEDEA   You mean, where all those fish are doing the backstroke?

MARY   Yes! That's it. Quite a wild place, I understand. It's only recently been colonised.

MEDEA   Oh good. I love an adventure.

MARY   Watch your landing gear, we're going down!

BOTH   Woooaahhh !

> *The wind blows very strong. Blackout. They 'crash land.' Wind fades into shopping mall muzak. Lights up. MARY and MEDEA appear with shopping bags from Holt Renfrew. MARY still has the suitcase. They exit together and MARY reappears immediately. She looks lost and panics. MEDEA enters, they 'find' each other and compare purchases: MARY has bought herself a blue veil and MEDEA has obtained a sword with an ornate belt. They exit together. Music changes to a suspense movie soundtrack. They reappear with bags of popcorn and 'watch' a movie. As they exit the sound changes again and the first video segment comes on.*
>
> *VIDEO #1: A YOUNG WOMAN PREPARES HER BATH, UNAWARE OF THE CAMERA. HER SURROUNDINGS ARE DULL AND ORDINARY, VERGING ON THE RUNDOWN. SHE MAKES THE NECESSARY PREPARATIONS, LIGHTS A CANDLE AND SHUTS THE DOOR AGAINST THE CAMERA. SCREEN TO BLACK.*

> *MARY and MEDEA appear USC with their shopping bags. They now wear their purchases. They look worn and bedraggled.*

MARY   God, I'm exhausted.

MEDEA   Gods, I'm absolutely worn out.

> *They sit and rest a moment. MARY begins to sniffle and weep.*

MEDEA   Oh, boo hoo hoo. *(pause)* Snap out of it, Mary. Mary!

> *MEDEA sneaks behind MARY and pulls a baby doll squeak toy out of MARY's shopping bag and squeaks it at her.*

MEDEA   The dingo et me bubby! The dingo et me bubby!

MARY   *(grabbing the toy)* How can you be so insensitive?

MEDEA   I'm not insensitive. I've just had it up to here with this sob-fest. Good gods above, I've never seen anyone go through so much woe.

MARY   And in so many accents.

MEDEA   "Roight." If I'd known how miserable things are down here, I'd never have come. Meryl Streep. Meryl Streep! What does she know about life?

MARY   She's wonderful. What strength. What fortitude. What expression!

MEDEA   She looked stunned half the time.

MARY   She was thinking, feeling, reacting. Gracefully!

MEDEA   Yes, she was. Thinking about how to get out of all those preposterous situations.

MARY   That's what life is like, Medea. *(pointedly getting the pronunciation right)* People find themselves in horrific situations that they have to get out of.

MEDEA   You're absolutely right. Do what you have to do and get over it.

MARY   Simple as that?

MEDEA   Simple as that.

MARY   You ought to know. *(pause)* I can't believe you sat right beside me watching those beautiful movies and you're so cold!

MEDEA   What am I supposed to be so upset about? *Heartburn?*

MARY   No, not that one. Jack Nicholson was a total cad, no woman would have put up with him.

MEDEA   Ah hah! Well? Well?

MARY   *A Cry In The Dark.*

MEDEA   Oh, don't get me started.

MARY   *Sophie's Choice.* Come on. You must have been able to identify with that one.

MEDEA   Alright, alright. *Sophie's Choice* was okay. But I didn't like the way the camera stuck on her face the whole time.

MARY   That was part of it, like a portrait.

MEDEA   No, it wasn't. It was more like the "Meryl Streep Show."

MARY   Well, I'm not going to argue with you about it, but it was like a portrait; I mean, who would have guessed what experience went into the making of that face? Anyway, I just think she's a really good actor.

MEDEA   Well, I guess she was sort of affecting in the part where she has to give up one of the kids. Choose between the boy and the girl, you know? I mean, how in Hades' foul name are you supposed to make a choice like that?

MARY   I know! And the little girl played that little flute in the train on the way to the concentration camp. *(pause)* I wonder why she picked the boy to live.

MEDEA   Well, he was older I guess, and stronger. Maybe she thought he'd have a better chance of surviving. Who cares? It's just a movie.

MARY   She was beside herself. She didn't know. She brought it all on herself, insisting that she was a Catholic and a Fascist. Sophie was an opportunist and it backfired on her.

MEDEA   Prove it.

> *The lights change. MARY drops to her knees and MEDEA pulls a swastika'd military hat and swagger stick out of her own shopping bag. They re-enact the "choice" scene from the movie.*

MARY   Please! Bitte! Bitte! I implore you. I'm not a Jew, I'm a Catholic! I tell you, my children and I, we don't belong here.

MEDEA   Zo. You're a Catholic. Zen you believe in der infinite mercy of Gott und in der life hereafter. Correct?

MARY   Ya, ya.

MEDEA   Vot did der Christ say? Didn't he say, "Suffer little kinder?" Hmmmm? "To come unto me?" Zo. You vill be doing von of your kinder a favour. Choose.

MARY   Vot? I don't understand. Vot do you mean?

MEDEA   It's very simple. Even a shtupid cow such as yourself ought to understand it. Ze boy or ze girl. Choose.

MARY   That's impossible! I can't choose.

MEDEA   Vell, if you don't, I'll send zem both to the left. Guards!

MARY   NO! Take her. Take my little girl! Oh, my God.

MEDEA   Ha ha ha! Murderer! Unnatural mother!

> *Sound and lights restored to scene. They put their props away.*

MARY   She had to pick the girl. She had to choose the sweetest and most fragile one to atone for her crime.

MEDEA   The amount of her expiation was directly proportionate to the size of her crime. She sank under the weight of all that guilt. Sank like a stone.

MARY   Right! That's why they showed her face like that. Because you'd never guess what was behind the mask. "And I of ladies most deject and wretched: Oh woe is me, to have seen what I have seen, and see what I see!"

MEDEA   And so, she killed herself?

MARY   Right!

MEDEA   Wrong.

> *Sound and lights change. Video on.*

> *VIDEO #2: THE SAME WOMAN, FULLY DRESSED AND MADE UP, LAYING AT THE BOTTOM OF THE BATHTUB. IT IS FILLED WITH WATER. NO BUBBLES ESCAPE HER NOSE OR MOUTH. THE ROOM NOW LOOKS ORNATE AND DECADENT, LINED WITH SATIN AND CANDELABRA. CAMERA ZOOMS IN TO CLOSEUP ON HER FACE AND FADE TO BLACK.*

> *MARY holds a cross aloft. MEDEA is crouched, feral. They inhabit separate spaces. Their monologues are intertwined.*

MEDEA   Forget Hamlet. It's me, Medea, standing on the blasted shore
         at the edge of time. Created by a man, I wasn't given the
         easy luxury of indecision or the dubious honour of a staged
         death. Harpie, harridan, most cruel and unnatural mother,
         witch, virago, she-wolf! These names and more have I been
         called because I dared take action. Where another would
         contemplate, I act. I excise my malignancy where another
         would pollute the state. I am a victim of Fate, the Gods and
         Euripides. All immodest passion and unreasoning force: I
         dared declare myself!

MARY   *Behold the Handmaid of the Lord; be it unto me according to
         Thy Word.* And I, perfect creation, ever meek, followed. To
         see reality swallowed into myth, myth into canonical law,
         law into subjugation. My icon on the standards of
         Crusaders, my image burned into mortified flesh at the
         Inquisition. My name the shackles that bind a thousand,
         million, countless women. This is your poison, your
         chancre. Impossible tyrant placed on the pillar of your
         suffering. What am I doing here? If I had been less perfect. If
         I had dared to declare!

                    *MARY throws down her cross and turns to
                    MEDEA.*

MARY   Then do it.

MEDEA   Do what?

MARY   Declare!

MEDEA   But, it's a myth.

MARY   Do it.

MEDEA   It will kill me.

MARY   NOW!

MEDEA   "Friends, now my course is clear: as quickly as possible
         To kill the children and then fly from Corinth: not
         Delay and so consign them to another hand
         To murder with a better will. For they must die
         In any case: and since they must, then I who gave

MEDEA   Them life will kill them. Arm yourself, my heart: the thing
         That you must do is fearful, yet inevitable.
         Why wait then? My accursed hand, come take the sword,
         Take it and forward to your frontier of despair.
         No cowardice, no tender memories; forget
         That you once loved them, that of your body they were born."

         MARY, as CHILD, comes to MEDEA.

MARY   *(as CHILD)* Mother...

MEDEA   "No! I won't — I can't do it. I'll think of it no more.
         I'll take them away. Why should I hurt them,
         To make their Father suffer, when I shall suffer
         Twice as much myself? I won't do it.
         I won't think of it again. *(pause)*
         Oh my heart, don't, don't don't do it!
         Oh miserable heart, let them be! Spare your children.
         They make you happy.
         And children's skin is soft, and their breath pure.
         I can't do it."

MARY   *(as MARY)* Medea...

MEDEA   "By all the fiends of hate in hell's depths, no!
         I'll not leave sons of mine to be the victims
         Of my enemies rage. Oh, this is horror.
         But anger strengthens my resolve."

MARY   *(as CHILD)* Mother, mother!

         *MEDEA stabs MARY/THE CHILD. MARY
         collapses. Video comes on.*

         *VIDEO #3: SETTING AS IN VIDEO #2.
         CLOSE IN ON WOMAN'S LEGS. BLOOD
         DRIPS ON THEM, SEEPING INTO BATH
         AND REDDENING WATER. PAN UP TO
         FACE, FADE TO BLACK.*

MEDEA   "For one short day, forget your children. Afterwards weep;
         Though you kill them, they were your beloved sons.
         Life has been cruel to me." *(keening)*

MARY   SHUT UP!

MEDEA   What?
                    Lights brighten.

MARY   I said, shut up. Medea, we'll have you no more. You hear
           that? No more Medea.

MEDEA   That was the myth. It wasn't me.

MARY   I don't care what it was. I've heard it again, and again, and
           again. Enough already! Do you hear? *(pause)* Look Medea, I
           don't mean to offend you, but you're always going on and
           on. Back over the same old ground. "Jason this, and Jason
           that." It's tiresome. You're becoming boring.

MEDEA   You put me through the same old bloodbath I've been forced
           to sit in all these years, then tell me I'm boring. That's very
           perverse. Excuse me.

                    *MEDEA gets MARY's shopping bag and
                    empties it on the floor. It's filled with baby
                    dolls. She pulls a hatchet out of her bag.*

MARY   Perverse or not, it's an open and shut case of self-
           immolation. Stop martyring yourself!

MEDEA   Faith has nothing to do with it. We're talking politics here,
           Mary. Drastic times require drastic measures. But then, you
           wouldn't know anything about secular problems.

                    *MEDEA kneels and lines the dolls up in front
                    of her.*

MARY   Do you think my life would have been like this if it weren't
           for Augustus Caesar? Do you think I had a good time being
           hauled all over Hell's HalfAcre? *(as MEDEA chops at a doll)*
           What are you doing?

MEDEA   Blowing off a little steam.

                    *MARY tries to reason with MEDEA who is
                    purposefully chopping away. She catches the
                    hurtling dolls and attempts to fix them.*

MARY	Listen to me! I was nine months pregnant for Christ's sake. Given a directive, with no choice, I ended up in a stable cozying up to livestock, and that was just the start of it.
MEDEA	You were just part of a happy set of circumstances that was engineered for a glorious outcome.
MARY	Get over it, Medea. Look at me. I've had much less time at this than you, and I'm coping. Take a look around! Get in touch with the world. There's more to you than you think.
MEDEA	Would you cut the self-help sophistry and get to the point?
MARY	I'm saying that you're captivated by this history you've been given. Look at you! You've bought your own publicity. The brave and regal sorceress who helps her man, hides her light behind him, and slays the kids in a fit of pique. You're infatuated with a myth. 'Woman of action.' 'Beacon of political injustice.' HAH! *(MARY has saved all the dolls)*
MEDEA	Oh, please! Look at at yourself. The meek and mild Queen of Heaven who rises above it all. Mary the dubious debutante with the mysteriously swollen belly. But God set Joseph straight about your divine dalliance. A religious rectification! I however, have no such out.
MARY	See. I told you. Going over the same territory. The same self-pity and loathing again. *(putting the dolls in the suitcase)*
MEDEA	Because I'm trapped! Caught in a place between crime and atonement, I am identifiable by my act alone. There is no out for me, no happy ending, no redemption. You will always give birth; and I will always kill the baby.
MARY	Ah yes. The suffering woman. Icon of action under duress. *(taking the hatchet and putting it in the suitcase)*
MEDEA	Yes, my action! I can't get past it. But then, how could you even begin to understand?
MARY	Pride, Medea. Many women suffer.

MEDEA   I'm not 'many women.' "I'd rather stand three times in the
        front line than bear one child." Yet I was a good mother,
        Mary. You must believe that.

MARY   You killed your children.

MEDEA   Yes, I did. I killed them. Didn't I tear out my own guts? But
        all I am is what people choose to see: Medea the Murderer.

MARY   You embrace it. Oh, you defy the pain and the grief, but in the
        end you need it. You feed on yourself. You're shrivelling up.

MEDEA   Yes, but I only damage myself. You, on the other hand,
        have a particularly sanguine legacy. Immaculate conception.
        Virgin birth.

MARY   The lies of legend. Don't you think I see it? Live with it?

MEDEA   And look what it's done for the world ever since. Look what
        you've done for women, with your immaculate, javexed
        birth process. The pose. The impossible meekness. Ah
        Mary, both our pedestals are built of blood.

MARY   That may be so. But at least I never called myself a victim
        of circumstance!

MEDEA   At least I stand defiant with my own blood on my hands!

MARY   Bullshit. Drop the monster. You are a woman, not a
        political statement. That's not why you acted. But over the
        years, that action has been turned around. Medea in the
        Twentieth Century is championed for the same reasons that
        condemned her 5,000 years ago.

MEDEA   I didn't choose to draw the knife. I had to. Things would
        have turned out so differently had I invented myself —
        invented the world I was created into.

MARY   Who is ever given that chance?

MEDEA   I stood unbowed before the storm and now lie covered with
        the debris of consequence. Buried alive. I want to sleep, but
        cannot. It's unfair.

MARY   Yes, it is unfair. But it's also tiresome.

MEDEA   It's all so tiresome. I'm not a butcher, not a beast, and
              certainly no champion of political injustice. I'm just trying
              to get by, like everybody else. Medea at the supermarket.
              Medea at the drugstore. Just trying to survive. Like you, and
              you, and you.

> *MARY is staring off to heaven, entranced.*

MEDEA   You, yoo-hoo...

> *MEDEA smiles and snaps her fingers. "Ave
> Maria" begins to play. MARY rises and floats
> beatifically. MEDEA watches then grabs her
> veil, dancing in a parody of MARY.*

MARY   Alright! You've made your point!

> *MARY grabs the veil back. The music
> abruptly ends.*

MEDEA   Earth to Mary! Earth to Mary!

MARY   I'm here!

MEDEA   Just testing.

MARY   I'll show you. I'll show you the real Medea.

> *Sound, light change. MEDEA sinks to the
> floor, the lights fade to a dim spot, catching
> MEDEA and the open suitcase. Video plays.*

> *VIDEO #4: THE WOMAN AS IN #2 AND
> #3. THE WATER IS NOT BLOODY. IT
> SWIRLS IN GENTLE EDDIES AROUND
> HER. LEAVES, TWIGS, AND DRIED
> PETALS FLOAT WITH THE SLOW
> MOTION OF THE WATER, OBSCURING
> THE WOMAN'S FACE. SLOW MOTION.
> FADE TO BLACK.*

> *MARY goes to the audience, holding her veil.*

MARY   Not too many miles away, there's a place where I once spent some time. On my daily rounds I walked up and down a street, and as I walked a certain corridor of the street I passed a restaurant on one side and a block of apartments on the other. Every day for years I passed by these two places and never gave either much thought. They were unremarkable; and so, never remarked upon.

Then one day I read in the local paper that some little boys playing in the dumpster behind the restaurant had found a suitcase. The case was locked; so, like normal boys, they pried it open. Inside they found a treasure beyond their wildest dreams.

It was the dried-up corpse of an infant. A baby that had been strangled at the age of three weeks. The forensic scientists said that it had been in the case for at least thirty years. You see, an old woman died in the apartment across the street. The landlady cleaned the unit out after discovering the body. She'd thrown everything away, including the suitcase stored under the bed. It all looked so insignificant.

The next day I paused in my walk down this unremarkable street. First I went to the restaurant and looked at the dumpster. Then I crossed the road and looked at the apartment building for a long time. I didn't know which window to look in. I just stared and thought of a woman.

I thought of a young woman who killed her baby. I wondered why. Didn't she love it? Or did she? What went wrong? Perhaps her lover left her and she was stranded. Crazy with grief and nowhere to turn. Poor woman, white trash. Forced to kill her child.

And then she slept with it under the bed for thirty years. How did she do that? The terror. Her personal atonement. A monstrous punishment to fit an unspeakable crime. Yet, in the end, so insignificant.

Although I continued my walk past it every day, that place was changed forever. In my mind, charged with unspoken accusation and remorse.

MEDEA rises slowly.

MEDEA "And children's skin is soft, and their breath pure." That was me, that old woman. That was me as a young mother. The one who, forced with a terrible choice, makes it. Faced with a monstrous action, takes it. There is no myth to it at all. Medea is around us everywhere. The monster walks the street — and in the end is just a woman. A survivor.

> *The video plays.*

> *VIDEO #5: THE WOMAN, NAKED AND GLEAMING, RISES FROM THE BATH. THE SATIN TRAPPINGS ARE GONE AND A LONE CANDLE BURNS. SHE TURNS AND LOOKS STRAIGHT AT THE CAMERA — THE AUDIENCE. FREEZE FRAME, THEN FADE TO BLACK.*

> *MARY and MEDEA throw the veil and the sword into the suitcase. MARY shuts and locks the case. A wind starts to blow. They grab their bags and begin to take off.*

MEDEA Hold it! What now?

MARY What do you mean?

MEDEA I mean, what's next? We don't have to go back, do we?

MARY Of course, we have to go back. Perhaps Meryl will be there.

MEDEA Maybe I'll finally get some sleep. Oh Gods, what luxury. To sleep!

MARY Perchance to dream...

MEDEA Shut up.

MARY Medea... *(getting it wrong, on purpose)*

MEDEA Medea! *(pause - then realizing)* Oh.

BOTH No more.

> *Blackout. The End.*